Crock-Pot Express Cookbook

Easy, Delicious, and Healthy Recipes for Your Crock-Pot Express Multi-Cooker

JANET COLE

Copyright 2018: Janet Cole - All rights reserved.

This document is geared towards providing exact and reliable information in regards to the topic and issue covered. The publication is sold with the idea that the publisher is not required to render accounting, officially permitted, or otherwise, qualified services. If advice is necessary, legal or professional, a practiced individual in the profession should be ordered.

- From a Declaration of Principles which was accepted and approved equally by a Committee of the American Bar Association and a Committee of Publishers and Associations.

In no way is it legal to reproduce, duplicate, or transmit any part of this document in either electronic means or in printed format. Recording of this publication is strictly prohibited and any storage of this document is not allowed unless with written permission from the publisher. All rights reserved.

The information provided herein is stated to be truthful and consistent, in that any liability, in terms of inattention or otherwise, by any usage or abuse of any policies, processes, or directions contained within is the solitary and utter responsibility of the recipient reader. Under no circumstances will any legal responsibility or blame be held against the publisher for any reparation, damages, or monetary loss due to the information herein, either directly or indirectly.

Respective authors own all copyrights not held by the publisher.

The information herein is offered for informational purposes solely, and is universal as so. The presentation of the information is without contract or any type of guarantee assurance.

The trademarks that are used are without any consent, and the publication of the trademark is without permission or backing by the trademark owner. All trademarks and brands within this book are for clarifying purposes only and are the owned by the owners themselves, not affiliated with this document.

Table of Contents

Introduction 1

Chapter 1: Introducing the Express Multi-Cooker 3

Chapter 2: Express Multi-Cooker Maintenance and Safety 11

Chapter 3: Using the Pressure Cooker Setting 17

Chapter 4: Breakfast 21
   Bacon 'n Egg Bake (Pressure Cooked) 22
   Meaty Egg Bake (Pressure Cooked) 24
   Classic Breakfast Casserole (Slow Cooked) 26
   Cheesy Potatoes (Slow Cooked) 28
   Vanilla-Bean Yogurt (Slow Cooked) 30
   Coconut-Lime Oats (Pressure Cooked) 32
   Fruity Steel-Cut Oats (Slow Cooked) 34
   Strawberry-Nutella French Toast (Slow Cooked) 36
   Orange-Iced Cinnamon Rolls (Slow Cooked) 38
   Raspberry French Toast (Pressure Cooked) 40

Chapter 5: Beef + Lamb 43
   Beef Bourguignon (Slow Cooked) 44
   Mongolian Beef (Slow Cooked) 46
   Beef Stroganoff (Pressure Cooked) 48
   Sesame-Ginger Short Ribs (Slow Cooked) 50
   Paprika-Chili Beef Brisket (Slow Cooked) 52
   Salisbury Steak (Pressure Cooked) 54
   Weeknight Steak 'n Potatoes (Slow Cooked) 56
   Beef-Potato Hash (Pressure Cooked) 58
   Simple Lamb Curry (Slow Cooked) 60
   Garlic Lamb Shanks (Pressure Cooked) 62

Chapter 6: Poultry 65
Teriyaki Chicken Sandwiches (Pressure Cooked)............66
Butter Chicken (Slow Cooked) 68
Chicken 'n Dumplings (Slow Cooked)............................70
Hawaiian BBQ Chicken (Pressure Cooked) 72
Chicken Cordon Bleu (Slow Cooked) 74
Easy Buffalo Chicken (Slow Cooked)..............................76
Salsa Verde Turkey + Rice (Pressure Cooked).................78
Turkey Breast w/ Gravy (Pressure Cooked)................... 80
Dijon Turkey + Gravy (Pressure Cooked)...................... 82
Thanksgiving Turkey (Slow Cooked) 84

Chapter 7: Pork 87
Honey-Ginger Pork Chops (Slow Cooked) 88
Honey-Mustard Pork Chops (Pressure Cooked)............. 90
Pork Roast w/ Maple Gravy (Slow Cooked).....................92
Pork Carnitas (Slow Cooked)..94
Blackberry-Cider Pork Loin (Pressure Cooked) 96
Coconut Milk-Braised Pork (Slow Cooked).................... 98
One-Pot Pork Chop Meal (Pressure Cooked) 100
Dr. Pepper Baby Back Ribs (Slow Cooked) 102
Beginner's Pork Belly (Pressure Cooked) 104
Classic Glazed Ham (Pressure Cooked)........................106

Chapter 8: Seafood.. 109
Easy Maple Salmon (Slow Cooked)............................... 110
Creamy Haddock + Spinach (Pressure Cooked)........... 112
Shrimp Boil (Slow Cooked) 114
Shrimp Paella (Pressure Cooked)................................ 116
Mussels, Rice, and Potatoes (Slow Cooked) 118
Spicy Garlic-Ginger Shrimp (Slow Cooked) 120
Shrimp Alfredo (Pressure Cooked)................................122
Quick Shrimp Risotto (Pressure Cooked)......................124
Sweet-Spicy Salmon (Slow Cooked)..............................126
Thai-Style Cod w/ Pineapple Salsa (Pressure Cooked).128

Chapter 9: Soups + Stews 131
Chicken Potato Soup (Slow Cooked)............................132
Lasagna Soup (Slow Cooked) 134

Beef Stew (Pressure Cooked)...136
Parmesan Chicken Soup (Slow Cooked).........................138
Chicken Noodle Soup (Pressure Cooked)......................140
Creamy Chicken + Wild Rice Soup (Slow Cooked).........142
Classic Tomato Soup (Pressure Cooked).......................144
Spiced Pumpkin Soup (Slow Cooked)............................146
Cheesy Cauliflower Soup (Pressure Cooked)................148
Clam Chowder (Pressure Cooked).................................150

Chapter 10: Vegan 153
Quinoa-Bean Chili (Slow Cooked)...................................154
Masala-Spiced Lentil Stew (Slow Cooked)....................156
Taco Bowl (Slow Cooked)...158
Minestrone Soup (Pressure Cooked).............................160
Butternut Squash + Spinach Risotto (Pressure Cooked)162
Tofu + Rice (Slow Cooked)...164
Coconut Tofu Curry (Pressure Cooked).........................166
Poached Pears (Pressure Cooked).................................168

Chapter 11: Sides + Snacks........................ 171
Buffalo Chicken Dip (Slow Cooked)................................172
Buffalo Chicken Wings (Pressure Cooked)...................174
Simple Spinach Dip (Slow Cooked)................................176
Hummus (Pressure Cooked)..178
Red-Wine Mushrooms (Slow Cooked)...........................180
Pork Pinto Beans (Pressure Cooked)............................182
Queso Dip (Slow Cooked)...184
Crab Party Dip (Slow Cooked)..186
Sweet 'n Sour Turkey Meatballs (Pressure Cooked).....188
Easy Veggie Rice (Pressure Cooked)............................190

Chapter 12: Condiments 193
Spaghetti Sauce (Slow Cooked)......................................194
Bolognese Sauce (Pressure Cooked)............................196
Homemade Ketchup (Slow Cooked)...............................198
Habanero Hot Sauce (Pressure Cooked).......................200
Serrano Relish (Slow Cooked)...202
Caramelized Onions (Pressure Cooked).......................204
Bacon Jam (Slow Cooked)..206

Maple-Chipotle BBQ Sauce (Pressure Cooked)............ 208

Chapter 13: Desserts.. 211
Chocolate Chip + Orange Scones (Slow Cooked)........... 212
Pumpkin Pie (Slow Cooked)..214
Apple-Pear Crisp (Slow Cooked) 216
Chocolate Molten Cake (Slow Cooked).........................218
Cinnamon-Raisin Bread Pudding (Slow Cooked) 220
Classic Cheesecake (Pressure Cooked) 222
Date-Night Fudge Cake (Pressure Cooked)...................225
Black 'n Blue Cobbler (Pressure Cooked) 227
Rich Lemon Custard (Pressure Cooked)........................ 229
Cider-Poached Pears w/ Cinnamon-Pecan Syrup (Pressure Cooked) 231

Epilogue 233

Introduction

Even if you enjoy it most days, cooking can be a chore. We live busy lives, and too often, preparing good food gets put by the wayside. How do you revive a love of cooking and keep it convenient? The Express Multi-Cooker from Crock-Pot is the answer.

The 8-in-1 Express Multi-Cooker lets you slow cook like a traditional Crock-Pot, but also pressure-cook, which has made brands like Instant Pot extremely successful. Pressure-cooking is when the boiling point of water gets raised, so cook times are dramatically slashed down. Foods that normally take a long time like steel-cut oats, stew, and so on can take less than 20-30 minutes. You now have the ability to choose between low and slow cooking that's done overnight or all day during work, or really fast cooking that you can do when you're running short on time.

This book explains everything you need to know about the Multi-Cooker, including the parts that make it different from a traditional Crock-Pot, and what the control panel programs mean. The cooker is equipped with a variety of safety features, so even when you're using the typically-riskier pressure cooker setting, you can feel confident and safe. There are still issues that come up, so I've also included a troubleshooting guide that addresses the most common problems.

For those who aren't familiar with pressure cooking, you'll also get step-by-step instructions on how to use that setting, and how to convert slow cooker recipes to pressure cooking. My goal is for you to feel comfortable going back and forth seamlessly between the two functions as convenience dictates! The Multi-Cooker is unlike any appliance you've used before, and I hope you love it and the recipes as much as I do.

Chapter 1: Introducing the Express Multi-Cooker

The Express Multi-Cooker from Crock-Pot, the original slow cooker brand, represents an exciting innovation in cooking appliances. You get both the traditional slow cooking method and pressure cooking, which has become popular in recent years. This chapter walks you through the history of both cooking methods, as well as what the Multi-Cooker is and why it's the new must-have kitchen gadget.

The history of the Crock-Pot

An old family recipe inspired the Crock-Pot. Irving Naxon's grandmother would reminiscence about "cholent," a Lithuanian beef-and-potato stew that took all day in the oven to cook. Naxon wanted to create an appliance that could replace the oven, and make cooking more convenient for people who worked all day. He released what he called the Naxon Beanery in the 1950's, and in 1970, it was renamed the Crock-Pot.

The Crock-Pot became very popular in the 1970's, when women worked outside the home more. They could start dinner in the morning, stick it in the Crock-Pot, and let it cook 8-10 hours, before returning home in the evening to finish up. Home cooks could also make breakfasts in the evening and cook it all through the night. At $25-$30, just about everyone could afford a slow cooker, and they became so popular that other companies began releasing their own versions. The name "Crock-Pot," however, came to describe all slow cookers.

By 2002, almost 81% of Americans owned a Crock-Pot, and advances in technology made them even more convenient and safe. The removable pot was one of the earliest innovations, and the most important, since it allowed users to wash the pot in the dishwasher. The Express Multi-Cooker represents the best technology that Crock-Pot has to offer, as you'll read later on.

The story of pressure cookers

Pressure cooking is based on the fact that the boiling point of water rises when pressure is allowed to build up. To accomplish this, the pot needs to have an airtight seal, so no pressure escapes. The first pressure cooker can be traced back to Denis Papin, who wanted to create a cooking device that could break down bones. He called it "the bone digester," and even prepared a meal for the French king. However, because it was so large and prone to explosions, it was never adopted by the masses.

It took another few centuries before anything close to the pressure cooker we know today was released. The invention of the cannery in the 19th century copied the airtight seal, but it was used for sealing jars of food, and not cooking meals. At the 1939 World's Fair, the first stove-top pressure cooker was presented, and during WWII, they became very popular. With less food and limited budgets, people relied more on gardens and cheaper cuts of meat. The pressure cooker was the best tool for breaking down tough meat and vegetables into nutritious soups and stews.

After the war, pressure cookers became less common as processed food took over. Pressure cookers were also still relatively dangerous, and just about everyone from that era has stories about cookers exploding spaghetti all the over the ceiling. In Asia, however, pressure cookers never went out of style, and companies based there continued to improve on the technology. The first electric cooker was patented in China in 1991, and in 2010, the first Instant Pot went to market. The Express Multi-Cooker represents Crock-Pot's first venture into this new world.

What is the Express Multi-Cooker?

So, what is this new device from Crock-Pot? It's a slow cooker *and* pressure cooker in one. That means it can cook food low and slow for hours at a time, or cook food really fast at high temperatures. The pot is 6-quarts, and it's dishwasher-safe. It's called the 8-in-1 because it has eight programs. To help you get a better idea of what this appliance can do, let's take a look at the parts and control panel:

The parts

The Multi-Cooker consists of a removable pot, a housing with a heating element, and the lid. The lid is the most unique part, because unlike a regular slow cooker, it has a silicone ring that allows for an airtight seal, and a pressure valve. The valve is a knob on top of the lid that is either in the "closed" or "venting" position. When you use the pressure cooker function, it should be in the "closed" position, since you need to contain the steam to build up pressure. When you're using the slow cooker function, the valve should be in the "venting" position.

The control panel

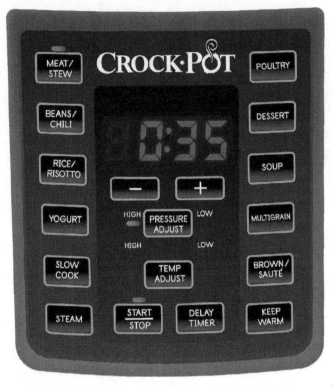

The control panel is where you operate the Multi-Cooker and select programs, cook times, and pressure. What do they all mean? Let's look at them in order:

MEAT/STEW - This pressure cooking setting is the default for meat and stew. It runs at high pressure for 35 minutes.

BEANS/CHILI - You'll see this setting used in the recipes, even when it isn't for beans. This is because the Multi-Cooker doesn't have a "Manual" setting; we use BEANS/CHILI instead because it has a wide time range. Without adjustment, this setting is 20 minutes on high pressure.

RICE/RISOTTO - This pressure cooking setting cooks at 12 minutes on low pressure.

YOGURT - Exclusive to making yogurt, it cooks at low temp for 8 hours, though you can adjust it from 6-12 hours.

STEAM - Another pressure cooking setting, it cooks at high pressure for 3 minutes to an hour. 3 minutes is the shortest possible time on the Multi-Cooker.

(+/-) - These buttons adjust cooking time, which is displayed as bright blue numbers. When you hit one of the cooking programs, the default time will pop up in the display screen, and you can adjust it with the (+/-) buttons.

PRESSURE ADJUST - Programs except STEAM can be adjusted to high or low pressure. You'll only use this when pressure cooking.

TEMP ADJUST - For the slow cooker function, you can choose between high or low heat.

START/STOP - You push this button to start a cooking cycle or stop it.

DELAY TIMER - This lets you delay a cooking cycle. You'll use the (+/-) buttons to input the time.

POULTRY - This setting automatically cooks at high pressure for 15 minutes.

DESSERT - This automatically cooks on low pressure for 10 minutes, though you can adjust to high pressure.

SOUP - You have both a low or high pressure option, though it cooks at high pressure automatically for 30 minutes.

MULTIGRAIN - The default is high pressure for 40 minutes, with the option for low pressure.

BROWN/SAUTÉ - This setting is used almost exclusively to prep various ingredients; it basically makes the Crock-Pot a skillet. This means you use it with the lid *off*. You'll see it used a lot in pressure cooking recipes.

KEEP WARM - When you want to keep your meal warm without cooking it further, this is the setting to use. The program lasts 4 hours before shutting off the cooker completely.

What are the Multi-Cooker's benefits?

With the Multi-Cooker, you basically get the benefits of both slow cookers and pressure cookers.

The Multi-Cooker is always convenient

Your schedule isn't always set in stone, and you need to be flexible with your time. Sometimes it's more convenient to cook something overnight or all day, and sometimes you just want to get a meal done in less than a half hour. The Multi-Cooker can do both, so it's always flexible with your schedule.

Pressure cooking is the healthiest cooking method

One of the benefits exclusive to pressure cooking is that it's the healthiest cooking method. Why? The longer food cooks, no matter what the temperature, the more nutrients leak into the cooking liquid. Unless you're eating the cooking liquid for every meal, there are lots of nutrients you miss out on. With pressure cooking, the cooking process is so fast that most of the nutrients are preserved in the food. According to studies, even somewhat heat-sensitive food like broccoli retains 90-95% of its original nutritional value.

Slow cooking is a one-step process

With slow cooking, there's always little to no prep. You don't even need to brown (most of the time); everything just goes in the pot at once. You don't need to worry about separate cooking times for different ingredients and timing things correctly. One-pot meals are very popular in our busy times, and that's what slow cookers were designed to do.

You can cook anything

In just one appliance, you can cook pretty much anything. There are foods that go straight into the pot like stew and soup, and others that use the bowl-in-pot method, where you basically use the cooker like an oven. With accessories like a trivet and steamer baskets, you can cook cakes, egg casseroles, and more. As you'll see in the recipes, you can cook any type of dish using either the slow cooker or pressure cooker functions.

The Multi-Cooker is easy to use

Even if you've never used a digital cooking appliance before, the Multi-Cooker is easy to learn. The buttons are there to help guide you, but as you'll see in the recipes, you really only use a few most of the time. Everything is clearly labeled, from the valve's "closed" or "venting" positions, to the food-max line marked in the pot. The Crock-Pot comes with an instruction book, but a lot of people don't even need it.

It's also safe

One of the big concerns about pressure cookers is that they're not safe, and even though Crock-Pot has been around for a while, some people are still nervous about leaving their slow cooker on when they're gone. The Multi-Cooker is equipped with all the necessary safety features. The Crock-Pot won't work in the pressure cooking setting unless the lid is sealed, and there are tiny holes in the lid to prevent too much pressure from building up. The Crock-Pot housing is also designed to stay cool, so no one gets burned bumping up against it, whether it's on the slow cooker setting or pressure cooking.

Chapter 2: Express Multi-Cooker Maintenance and Safety

Keeping appliances clean is a big part of ensuring their longevity. The Multi-Cooker is no exception. The removable pot needs to be washed after every meal. It's dishwasher-safe, and it can be cleaned with a soft sponge, warm water, and soap. Abrasive sponges will scratch the surface, so don't use those. The housing can get dirty, too, and can be cleaned easily with just water and a paper towel. There's also a plastic condensation collector that can be emptied and rinsed out when necessary.

The lid of the Multi-Cooker is the other part that you really need to keep clean. If it gets too dirty, various valves and what not can get clogged, and the cooker won't work properly. The sealing ring that provides the airtight seal (also called the gasket) is removable and should be washed every 2-3 times you use the cooker. It absorbs smells, so you might need to wash it more frequently if you're cooking strong-smelling ingredients like onions and tomatoes. You can run it through the dishwasher, or wash it by hand with warm water and soap. It the smells don't go away after a good wash, soak it in a mixture of water, baking soda, and vinegar. Always dry it well before putting it back into the lid. Over time, gaskets wears down, crack, and lose their airtight seal. Every 2-3 years, you'll need to buy a new one.

As you use your Multi-Cooker, the steam release valve can get clogged. To clean it, you can actually pop it off and clean the hole with a knitting needle or something else long and unbreakable. If you use water, air-dry really well. The other part you want to clean is the valve *cover*, which is on the inside of the lid. It's covered by a metal cap (see image to the right), which can be popped off - not twisted off - and rinsed out.

Using the Multi-Cooker safely

The Multi-Cooker is safe to use, thanks to the features built into the appliance. The slow cooker function is safer than the pressure cooker one, simply because pressure isn't building up and the temperatures are lower. To use the slow cooker setting safely, always make sure the pressure valve is in the "open" or "venting" position. This allows any steam to escape, and not build up.

When you're using the pressure cooker setting, you don't have to worry about explosions, but you should be most careful when you're releasing the pressure. Recipes will tell you to either wait for a natural pressure release when a cooking cycle is over, or "quick-release" the pressure. Quick-release means you open the valve manually, allowing the steam to escape. That steam is hot, so you should always keep your face away from it, and watch your hands.

Before using the Multi-Cooker at all, make sure the parts are all assembled correctly, and that they're dry. When you add food, don't fill past the "max" line. When your meal is eaten and it's time to clean up, unplug the cooker.

Troubleshooting the Multi-Cooker

So, you're using your Multi-Cooker to cook a fantastic meal, but something is going wrong. There are issues that can pop up when you're using either the slow cooker function or the pressure cooker one. Here's how to deal with the most frequently-cited problems:

Slow cooker

Food that's burned or unevenly cooked is common when slow cooking, while a meal with too much liquid at the end or a smoking pot also occurs.

Burned food

If you realize something has burned while cooking on the slow cooker function, it's probably going to be something a bit delicate, like a vegetable. You can quickly solve this problem in the future by adding an insert or lining the pot with foil. This prevents the food from making direct contact with the hot stainless-steel.

Unevenly cooked food

A common issue with stews, you've ended up with mushy vegetables and well-cooked meat. Or, your potatoes are still hard, while other ingredients are fine. To prevent uneven cooking, you want to make sure vegetables that cook quickly are cut into larger sizes than meat, to balance out the timing. For potatoes and other ingredients that seem to take longer, cut into smaller pieces. As a general rule, the bigger the cut, the longer it takes to cook. You can also add ingredients later in the cooking process, which is recommended for vegetables that are already cooked, and just frozen.

Too much liquid

You've finished cooking a meal, but there's too much liquid. An easy fix right away is to turn your cooker to BROWN/SAUTÉ and cook off the excess. In the future, simply add less liquid. Remember that slow cooking doesn't result in a lot of evaporation, and if a recipe doesn't require any liquid, don't be tempted to put some in. Vegetables and meat render their own liquids, so they don't cook "dry" and burn.

The cooker is smoking

Smoke usually occurs when you first turn on your Multi-Cooker. This nearly always means that there's food or oil in the cooker, or right by the heating element. Before attempting any fix, turn off the cooker and wait for it to cool. Once cool, you can clean the pot and the bottom of the cooker.

Pressure cooker

Using the pressure cooker setting can result in six problems, and the fixes are different than with the slow cooker.

The Multi-Cooker won't reach pressure

You're ready to use the pressure cooker setting, but the pressure won't build. The first thing to do is check the gasket and make sure it's fitted properly. If there are any tears or it seems loose, you'll need a new one. The other solution is to make sure the pressure valve is in the "closed" position.

Water or steam leaks out

The Multi-Cooker is doing its thing, and you notice water or steam leaking from the pressure valve. This is likely because something somewhere is blocked, and the cooker needs a good clean. Check the valve and hit the bobber valve a few times (the little pin that pops up when the cooker is full of pressure, and goes down when there's no pressure). The gasket might also be too loose, so check that, and get a new one if it's too old.

Water or food sprays out when you release pressure

The timer went off and you turn the pressure release valve, only to have water or food spraying out. This tends to happen with "frothy" foods like beans and rice. Basically, anything with starch can cause spraying. You will want to wait for a natural pressure release with foods like this, and if the recipe calls for that type of release, you should obey. That time is sometimes needed to finish cooking, as well as prevent spraying. If you are following the instructions for a quick-release and spraying still occurs, you might have filled the cooker too full. Always make sure to stay at or below that max line.

The lid is stuck

If the lid to the Multi-Cooker won't come off after you've released the pressure, it's because there's still pressure trapped inside. The stuck lid is a safety precaution. Check to make sure the valve is turned to all the way open, and if that doesn't work, you can actually pull it off. Turn the cooker on to BROWN/SAUTÉ or another setting, and that should push all the pressure out.

Food is undercooked

Undercooked food with the pressure cooker setting almost always happens because you used too much liquid. This is common, because pressure cooking uses less liquid than slow cooking. You basically only need ½ cup for any recipe to generate the steam necessary to build pressure. If a recipe doesn't require a liquid, it's because the ingredients will create their own. Filling the cooker too full can also result in undercooking. With the pressure cooker setting, you definitely shouldn't fill above the max line. In fact, as little as ½ way full is recommended for foods that expand, like rice, pasta, and oatmeal.

Tried those solutions? The problem might be your actual ingredients. Frozen vegetables and meat need to cook longer than their thawed variations, while thickeners like flour and cornstarch can affect the doneness of the meal. Add thickeners *after* you've released pressure. To fix an undercooked meal, simply return the cooker to LOW pressure for 3-5 minutes, or if you think that would be too long, hit BROWN/SAUTÉ and finish cooking with the lid off. This way you can monitor the food's doneness more closely.

Food is overcooked

Overcooking the food is common if you haven't used a pressure cooker before. Because the cooking times are so much shorter than with other methods, people tend to think they need to add time. With such high temperatures, even a few minutes can have a big effect on food. To prevent overcooking, always follow the time recommended by the recipe. It's always better to undercook something anyway, because it's an easy fix. Overcooked food can't be saved. If your food is burning, you probably need to use a trivet or steamer basket. Trivets set down in the pot, and food is either put in a bowl or wrapped in foil, and set on top. Steamer baskets hang above the bottom of the pot, and are used for vegetables and fish.

Chapter 3: Using the Pressure Cooker Setting

We've described the Express Multi-Cooker in detail and why it's such a great appliance to have, but you might still be skeptical about the pressure cooking part. How do you use it exactly? And what about all the slow cooker recipes you already know and love? Can you speed those up using the pressure cooker function on the Multi-Cooker?

Pressure cooking step-by step

A lot of people are intimidated by pressure cookers because they seem complicated. However, they're really easy to get the hang of once you know the basics terms like "quick-release" and how to use the different buttons on the Multi-Cooker to make the best meals. Here's a walkthrough of a typical recipe:

Step 1: Prepping ingredients

This is when you do any chopping, slicing, peeling, and so on. With a lot of pressure cooker recipes, you'll be told to sauté or brown certain ingredients in a little oil. Aromatics like onion, garlic, celery, carrots, and spices are the most common. This helps build layers of flavor that would otherwise take a long time to create. You will sometimes be asked to "deglaze" the pot, which means pouring in a liquid like stock or wine, and scraping up any burnt food bits. This part has you treat the cooker like a skillet, so the lid remains off.

Step 2: Sealing the lid and selecting a time/pressure

The ingredients you're pressure cooking are now all in the pot. You seal the lid, which means putting on the lid properly and closing the pressure valve, so pressure can't escape. You now have to choose a cooking time and pressure. In this book, you nearly always choose BEANS/CHILI. There isn't really a reason for it, you could just as easily choose MEAT/STEW, because you will be adjusting the time manually anyway. As soon as you hit one of the programs, the time pops up in the display screen. Using the (+/-) buttons, you get to the time given in the recipe. If the pressure is supposed to be LOW, hit the PRESSURE ADJUST button. A blue light should go on above LOW. Now, hit START. This instruction isn't in the recipes; it's assumed that you press it.

Step 3: Pressure release

When time is up, the timer beeps. You'll now either wait for a natural pressure release, or quick-release. If you're waiting, you can tell when the pressure is gone because the little bobber valve pin sinks down. You can also move the pressure valve towards "open," and if no steam comes out, it's safe to open the lid. Sometimes you'll be told to wait 5-10 minutes for a natural pressure release, and *then* quick-release.

Step 4: Additional cooking

Depending on the recipe, it's now ready to serve as soon as you open the lid, or there are additional steps. This is usually the time when you add any thickeners. You also add dairy, because dairy doesn't do well when it's pressure cooked. The recipe might tell you to hit BROWN/SAUTÉ again, or keep the cooker at KEEP WARM. You most likely keep the lid off during this time.

And that's how you pressure cook! The control panel might look intimidating, but it's all pretty self-explanatory, and you only use a few buttons per recipe. If you're worried you messed something up on the control panel, you can always unplug the cooker and start again.

Converting recipes from slow cooking to pressure cooking

If you're like most people, you've used a Crock-Pot before, and you have favorite recipes. Now that you have a pressure cooker, too, you might want to convert those favorites. There are three actions you take to turn a slow cooked recipe into a pressure cooked one:

Cook certain ingredients on BROWN/SAUTÉ

Most slow cooker recipes don't have a step where you cook any ingredients before closing up the lid. With pressure cooking, however, that sauteéing builds more flavor into the finished product. Look at the ingredient list of your slow cooker recipe and pick out aromatics. These will include onion, garlic, carrots, celery, herbs, and whole spices. You can also brown meats like pork, chicken, and beef beforehand.

Reduce the amount of liquid

Slow cooked recipes use more liquid than pressure cooked ones, because there's evaporation. No liquid is lost during pressure cooking, however, because of that airtight seal. You want to *reduce* the liquid so you don't risk undercooking the meal. To figure out how much to use, decide how much liquid you want in the finished meal. That's what you'll put in. For dishes like oatmeal, rice, and pasta, you usually only need enough liquid to just cover the ingredients.

You might need to actually add liquid in some cases, if the slow cooker recipe doesn't call for any. At least ½ cup is usually required for a pressure cooker to generate steam. If you believe the recipe's ingredients will generate their own liquid, but you aren't sure, add just a tablespoon or so of liquid.

Reduce cooking time

Lastly, pick a cooking time. It will be significantly less than the slow cooker one. As a general rule, you pressure cook for less than 10% of the slow cooking time. You can also look at a comparable recipe online specifically for pressure cookers and see what time it recommends.

Chapter 4: Breakfast

You've probably heard "Breakfast is the most important meal of the day" enough times that it's lost all meaning, so let's not bother with all the nutritional reasons why eating after you wake up is important. Mornings can be stressful. There's last-minute chores you've put off or just remembered, and if you have a family, they're all running slower and not thinking about the kind of food that's going into their body. The Multi-Cooker lets you either cook breakfast the night before, when you are still sharp, or cook a really quick breakfast that you can do half-asleep. In this section, you'll find recipes for a variety of egg bakes and casseroles, as well as decadent French toasts and cinnamon rolls that are perfect for weekends, when you can actually take a bit more time in the kitchen.

Bacon 'n Egg Bake (Pressure Cooked)............................. 22
Meaty Egg Bake (Pressure Cooked).................................. 24
Classic Breakfast Casserole (Slow Cooked) 26
Cheesy Potatoes (Slow Cooked)... 28
Vanilla-Bean Yogurt (Slow Cooked) 30
Coconut-Lime Oats (Pressure Cooked) 32
Fruity Steel-Cut Oats (Slow Cooked)................................... 34
Strawberry-Nutella French Toast (Slow Cooked)............. 36
Orange-Iced Cinnamon Rolls (Slow Cooked)................... 38
Raspberry French Toast (Pressure Cooked)...................... 40

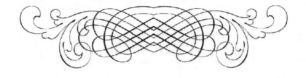

Bacon 'n Egg Bake (Pressure Cooked)

Serves: 4

Prep time: 10 minutes
Cook time: 20 minutes
Total time: 30 minutes

Bacon and eggs is the classic American breakfast, and in this recipe, it gets an upgrade with hash browns and plenty of cheese. Since this recipe is pressure cooked, it requires a bowl-in-pot method. This means you fill the Crock-Pot with water, and then set a bowl with the ingredients inside on a trivet. The Multi-Cooker basically acts like a steamer and cooks the bake.

Ingredients:

1 ½ cups water

6 chopped bacon slices
1 diced onion
2 cups frozen hash browns
6 eggs
¼ cup whole milk
¼ cup shredded cheddar cheese
¼ cup shredded mozzarella cheese
1 teaspoon garlic powder
Salt to taste
Black pepper to taste

Instructions:

1. Pour water into your Crock-Pot.
2. In a skillet, cook bacon and onion until crispy and golden.

3. Add in hash browns and stir around until they're beginning to thaw.
4. In another bowl, whisk eggs, milk, cheese, and seasonings together.
5. Stir in bacon/hash brown mixture.
6. Grease another bowl that is pressure cooker safe. This will be the shape of your bake.
7. Put a trivet into your Crock-Pot and set bowl on top.
8. Seal the lid.
9. Hit BEANS/CHILI and cook on high pressure for 20 minutes.
10. When time is up, quick-release. Make sure bake is 160-degrees.
11. Remove bake from bowl and serve!

Nutritional Info (¼ recipe):
Total calories: 307
Protein: 21
Carbs: 15
Fat: 16
Fiber: 2

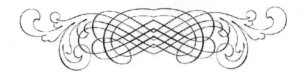

Meaty Egg Bake (Pressure Cooked)

Serves: 4

Prep time: 5 minutes
Cook time: 30 minutes
Total time: 35 minutes

With three kinds of meat, this is definitely not a vegan dish. Prep time is really quick at just 5 minutes. You mix everything in a bowl, wrap loosely in foil, and put in your Crock-Pot for 30 minutes. The bake should slide out of the bowl like a cheesy, meaty cake, and it's ready to eat!

Ingredients:

1 cup water

6 eggs
½ cup whole milk
Salt to taste
Black pepper to taste
4 slices cooked and chopped bacon
1 cup cooked ground beef
½ cup diced Canadian bacon
1 cup shredded Mexican cheese

Instructions:

1. Pour water into your Crock-Pot.
2. In a bowl, mix eggs, milk, and seasonings.
3. Stir in the meats and cheese.
4. Pour into a greased pressure cooker safe dish.
5. Cover loosely with foil and set on a trivet in the Crock-Pot.

6. Seal the lid.
7. Cook on BEANS/CHILI for 30 minutes on high pressure.
8. When time is up, quick-release. Bake should be at least 160-degrees.
9. Serve hot!

Nutritional Info (¼ recipe):
Total calories: 381
Protein: 30
Carbs: 3
Fat: 26
Fiber: 0

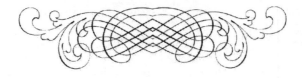

Classic Breakfast Casserole (Slow Cooked)

Serves: 6

Prep time: 10 minutes
Cook time: 6-8 hours
Total time: 6 hours, 10 minutes – 8 hours, 10 minutes

When you don't want to cook breakfast in the morning, this is the recipe to turn to. It takes 6-8 hours, which means it cooks overnight while you get your beauty sleep. With hash browns, pork sausage, cheese, and lots of seasonings, you can feed up to six people with the casserole, or have leftovers.

Ingredients:

8 eggs
¾ cup whole milk
½ teaspoon onion powder
½ teaspoon paprika
Salt to taste
Black pepper to taste
4 ½ cups hash browns
8-ounces cooked and sliced pork sausage
1 ½ cups shredded cheddar cheese
4 chopped scallions

Instructions:

1. Grease your Crock-Pot or put in an insert.
2. In a bowl, mix eggs, milk, and seasonings.
3. Lay down ⅓ of the hash browns in your Crock-Pot, then add ⅓ of

the sausage, scallions, and cheese. Keep repeating this until you end with cheese.
4. Pour in the egg mixture.
5. Close the lid.
6. Hit SLOW COOK and cook on low for 6-8 hours.
7. Make sure casserole is at least 160-degrees.
8. Serve!

Nutritional Info (⅙ recipe):
Total calories: 654
Protein: 27
Carbs: 45
Fat: 40
Fiber: 3

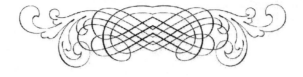

Cheesy Potatoes (Slow Cooked)

Serves: 8

Prep time: 5 minutes
Cook time: 4-5 hours
Total time: 4 hours, 5 minutes – 5 hours, 5 minutes

Breakfast potatoes are a hearty breakfast that's perfect before or after a good workout. Or, on a day where you just need a carbo load, because why not? Cooked with bell peppers, onion, and summer sausage, these potatoes are anything but one-note, and the addition of sour cream and cream of chicken soup ensures a delicious creaminess I can't get enough of.

Ingredients:

4 pounds diced Yukon Gold potatoes
2 diced yellow bell peppers
1 diced onion
1 sliced summer sausage
1 ½ cups shredded cheddar cheese
½ cup sour cream
1 (10.5-ounce) cream of chicken soup
1 teaspoon Italian seasoning
Salt to taste
Black pepper to taste

Instructions:

1. Grease or line your Crock-Pot.
2. Put all the ingredients in the pot, stirring well.
3. Hit SLOW COOK and cook on LOW for 4-5 hours.
4. Serve hot!

Nutritional Info (⅛ recipe):
Total calories: 475
Protein: 18
Carbs: 60
Fat: 21
Fiber: 7

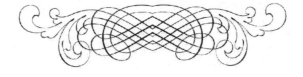

Vanilla-Bean Yogurt (Slow Cooked)

Serves: 8-10

Prep time: 30 minutes
Cook time: 10 hours
Chill time: 8 hours
Total time: 18 hours, 30 minutes

Homemade yogurt takes a while, but it's worth it. It's so much healthier and you can flavor it any way you want. This recipe is for a very basic vanilla-bean yogurt that uses both vanilla extract and vanilla beans. First, you heat milk to 180-degrees, and then cool it down right away. The yogurt starter goes in, which is just any store-bought plain yogurt that has active live cultures. Add vanilla flavoring and cook on the YOGURT setting for the next 10 hours. The waiting game will have to continue after time is up; the yogurt sits in the fridge for 8 hours before it's ready.

Cooking Note: The YOGURT setting goes up to 12 hours. The longer you choose, the less tart the yogurt is.

Ingredients:

½ gallon whole milk
2 tablespoons yogurt starter
2 tablespoons pure vanilla extract
Scraped beans from 2 vanilla pods

Instructions:

1. Pour milk into your Crock-Pot and close the lid.
2. Hit YOGURT and select HIGH temperature.
3. Whisk during the heating process, checking the temperature

4. frequently as well.
4. You want the milk to hit 180-degrees.
5. Fill your sink with cold water.
6. Carefully move Crock-Pot and set in the sink without letting water into the pot.
7. Cool milk down to at least 105-degrees, whisking frequently.
8. Spoon out a little milk into a separate bowl, and whisk in the yogurt starter.
9. Pour back into the pot and keep stirring until it's all blended.
10. Dry off the bottom of the Crock-Pot, and return to its spot atop the heating element.
11. Mix in the vanilla beans and vanilla extract.
12. Hit YOGURT again, adjusting the temperature to LOW this time, and adjust time to 10 hours.
13. When time is up, you'll move the pot and put it in the fridge, covered with foil.
14. Wait 8 hours before eating.

Nutritional Info (⅛ recipe):

Total calories: 150
Protein: 8
Carbs: 11
Fat: 8
Fiber: 0

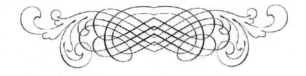

Coconut-Lime Oats (Pressure Cooked)

Serves: 4

Prep time: 1 minute
Cook time: 10 minutes
Natural pressure release: 10 minutes
Total time: 21 minutes

Coconut and lime are a tropical flavor pairing made in heaven. They're the perfect lightly sweet-nutty-tart addition to creamy steel-cut oats, which cook in full-fat coconut milk for just 10 minutes in the Crock-Pot. I could eat these oats for dessert, they're so good, but they're guilt-free, so I feel totally fine devouring them for breakfast, too.

Ingredients:

1 cup dry steel-cut oats
1 cup full-fat coconut milk
2 ½ cups water
Pinch of salt
¼ cup shredded coconut
2 teaspoons lime zest
Honey to taste

Instructions:

1. Grease your Crock-Pot well.
2. Pour oats, milk, and water into the cooker.
3. Hit BEANS/CHILI and adjust time to 10 minutes.
4. When time is up, turn off Crock-Pot and let the pressure come down naturally.
5. Oats may appear liquidy- stir, and then they thicken.

6. Serve with coconut, lime zest, and a little honey!

Nutritional Info (¼ recipe):
Total calories: 318
Protein: 6
Carbs: 49
Fat: 12
Fiber: 4

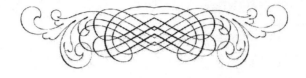

Fruity Steel-Cut Oats (Slow Cooked)

Serves: 8

Prep time: 1 minute
Cook time: 8 hours
Total time: 8 hours, 1 minute

Love berries? Then this is the breakfast for you. Steel-cut oats are cooked in water, coconut milk, and butter, and then topped with a mixture of raspberries, blueberries, and blackberries. They can be fresh or frozen. To sweeten, add a little honey. This recipe can cook all night while you sleep.

Ingredients:

2 cups dry steel-cut oats
6 cups water
2 cups unsweetened coconut milk (like Silk)
2 tablespoons butter
1 tablespoon cinnamon
1 cup raspberries
1 cup blueberries
½ cup blackberries
Honey to taste

Instructions:

1. Grease your Crock-Pot well.
2. Put all the ingredients in the pot, and close the lid.
3. Hit SLOW COOK and adjust time to 8 hours on LOW.
4. When time is up, stir the oatmeal.

5. Add berries and sweetener!

Nutritional Info (⅛ recipe):
Total calories: 199
Protein: 6
Carbs: 33
Fat: 7
Fiber: 5

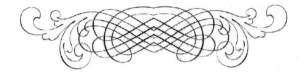

Strawberry-Nutella French Toast (Slow Cooked)

<u>Serves:</u> 8

Prep time: 12 minutes
Cook time: 2 hours
Total time: 2 hours, 12 minutes

Serving breakfast to a special somebody? This is the perfect French toast recipe for your Multi-Cooker. You want a nice sturdy bread, so when it soaks in milk, eggs, and Nutella for 10 minutes, it doesn't become too mushy. Cook for two hours on SLOW COOK, and then serve with skillet-softened strawberries!

<u>Ingredients:</u>

1 pound cubed sturdy bread (like challah)
6 eggs
2 cups whole milk
2 tablespoons Nutella
1 tablespoon pure vanilla
1 teaspoon cinnamon
Pinch of sea salt
10 fresh sliced strawberries
1 tablespoon white sugar
1 tablespoon butter

<u>Instructions:</u>

1. Put your bread in the Crock-Pot.
2. In a bowl, mix eggs, milk, Nutella, vanilla, cinnamon, and salt.

3. Pour over the bread, stir, and soak for 10 minutes.
4. Close the lid.
5. Hit SLOW COOK and cook on high for 2 hours.
6. When there's 15 minutes or so left on the timer, mix strawberries and white sugar together in a bowl.
7. Add butter to a skillet and melt.
8. Add sugared strawberries to melted butter and cook for 2 minutes or so, stirring.
9. To serve, spoon strawberry mixture on top of Nutella French toast!

Nutritional Info (⅛ recipe):
Total calories: 509
Protein: 18
Carbs: 71
Fat: 17
Fiber: 1.5

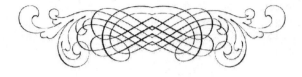

Orange-Iced Cinnamon Rolls (Slow Cooked)

Serves: 10-12

Prep time: 25 minutes
Cook time: 2 hours
Total time: 2 hours, 25 minutes

Cinnamon rolls are a guilty pleasure for me. I'm always looking for an excuse to make them. These are ideal for Christmas morning, but I can justify making them for just about any occasion. The dough is the standard milk, yeast, sugar, salt, butter, egg, and flour mixture, while the filling is also the normal butter, sugar, and cinnamon mix. Why mess with perfection? The glaze is what I really love. You use both orange juice and orange zest, so that flavor really comes through.

Ingredients:

¾ cup whole milk
2 ¼ teaspoons instant yeast
¼ cup (+1 teaspoon) white sugar
1 teaspoon salt
3 tablespoons melted butter
1 egg
2 ¾ cups whole-wheat flour
5 tablespoons soft butter
1 tablespoon ground cinnamon
⅓ cup white sugar
2 cups powdered sugar
¼ cup orange juice
3 tablespoons whole milk
3 teaspoons orange zest

Pinch of salt

Instructions:

1. Make the dough first. Warm milk until it's at a lukewarm temp, and then pour into your heavy mixer.
2. By hand, stir in yeast and 1 teaspoon sugar.
3. Wait 5-10 minutes until yeast foams.
4. On the low speed, beat in ¼ cup sugar, salt, butter, egg, and 2 cups of flour.
5. Gradually add in the rest of the flour ¼ cup at a time, until the dough becomes soft with an elastic texture.
6. Flour a cutting board and knead dough by hand for 2 minutes.
7. Rest for 10 minutes.
8. Now for the filling. Roll out dough into a rectangle.
9. Brush butter.
10. Mix cinnamon and sugar, then sprinkle evenly on top of buttered dough.
11. Roll up as tight as you can.
12. With a sharp, wet knife, cut into 10-12 pieces. These are your rolls!
13. Put inside your well-greased (or lined) Crock-Pot.
14. Put a paper towel on top before closing lid.
15. Cook on SLOW COOK for 2 hours on the high setting.
16. To make your glaze, simply whip all the ingredients together.
17. To serve, drizzle rolls with glaze and enjoy!

Nutritional Info (1/10 recipe):
Total calories: 355
Protein: 6
Carbs: 61
Fat: 11
Fiber: 2.5

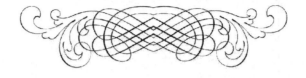

Raspberry French Toast (Pressure Cooked)

Serves: 8

Prep time: 15 minutes
Cook time: 25 minutes
Total time: 40 minutes

For a really quick French Toast recipe that's still impressive, I like throwing together this recipe in the Crock-Pot, and cook on the pressure cooking setting. It cooks in a cake pan atop a trivet, so remember to pour in that 1 cup of water into the Crock-Pot right away. A sturdy bread like Challah is ideal. The topping, which doesn't cook in the Multi-Cooker, is raspberries, orange juice, sugar, cinnamon, and a pinch of salt. Smash those together, heat in a skillet, and the juices and sugar blend together beautifully.

Ingredients:

1 cup water
4 tablespoons melted butter
½ cup sugar
2 cups whole milk
3 eggs
1 tablespoon pure vanilla
Pinch of salt
1 cubed loaf of sturdy bread
2 cups fresh raspberries
¼ cup orange juice
½ cup sugar
Pinch of cinnamon
Pinch of salt

Instructions:

1. Pour 1 cup water into your Crock-Pot.
2. In a bowl, mix butter, sugar, milk, eggs, vanilla, and salt.
3. Put your bread in a large bowl, and pour over the liquid mixture.
4. Soak for 10 minutes.
5. Pour in a greased cake pan that you know fits in the cooker.
6. Lower trivet into the Crock-Pot and set the French toast pan on it.
7. Seal the lid.
8. Hit BEANS/CHILI and adjust time to 25 minutes on high pressure.
9. Put the ingredients in the second list in a bowl, and smash a little with the back of a spoon.
10. Heat in a skillet for a few minutes, until berries begin to bubble and thicken.
11. When the Crock-Pot beeps, quick-release the pressure.
12. Serve French toast with raspberries on top!

Nutritional Info (⅛ recipe):

Total calories: 572
Protein: 13
Carbs: 94
Fat: 16
Fiber: 3

Chapter 5: Beef + Lamb

Beef and lamb - the other red meat - are perfect proteins for both slow cooking and pressure cooking. They tend to be a bit tougher, and both cooking methods are excellent at breaking down the toughest cuts and melting fat, so the meals end up fork-tender and mouthwatering. In this section, you'll find both slow and fast recipes for classics like beef stroganoff, Salisbury steak, and lamb shanks. Spices are important for variety, so expect to experience flavors like paprika, sesame, and ginger. It's exciting!

Beef Bourguignon (Slow Cooked) 44
Mongolian Beef (Slow Cooked) 46
Beef Stroganoff (Pressure Cooked) 48
Sesame-Ginger Short Ribs (Slow Cooked) 50
Paprika-Chili Beef Brisket (Slow Cooked) 52
Salisbury Steak (Pressure Cooked) 54
Weeknight Steak 'n Potatoes (Slow Cooked) 56
Beef-Potato Hash (Pressure Cooked) 58
Simple Lamb Curry (Slow Cooked) 60
Garlic Lamb Shanks (Pressure Cooked) 62

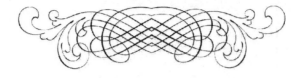

Beef Bourguignon (Slow Cooked)

Serves: 6

Prep time: 10 minutes
Cook time: 8-10 hours
Total time: 8 hours, 10 minutes – 10 hours, 10 minutes

A classic French dish from Burgundy, France, this beef stew is simmered for 8-10 hours in red wine and chicken stock. There are potatoes in there, too, so the stew is really hearty and sure to fill up even the emptiest stomach. You prep the ingredients (browning and deglazing) in a skillet, and then everything ends up in the Crock-Pot.

Ingredients:

3 pounds cubed boneless beef chuck
Salt to taste
Black pepper to taste
Glug of extra-virgin olive oil
1 cup red wine
2 cups chicken stock
½ cup tomato sauce
¼ cup soy sauce
¼ cup flour
1 pound Yukon gold potatoes
5 sliced carrots
3 minced garlic cloves
Italian seasoning to taste

Instructions:

1. Season beef with salt and pepper.
2. Pour oil into a skillet and heat.
3. When hot, sear the beef all over.
4. Grease your Crock-Pot while the meat cooks.
5. When browned, add beef to Crock-Pot.
6. Pour red wine into the skillet and deglaze by scraping up any stuck-on beef bits.
7. Simmer until a bit reduced, then add chicken broth, tomato sauce, and soy sauce.
8. Whisk in flour until smooth, then pour into Crock-Pot.
9. Add the rest of the ingredients into the Crock-Pot and stir.
10. Cook on SLOW COOK on the low setting for 8-10 hours.
11. Serve hot!

Nutritional Info (⅙ recipe):
Total calories: 637
Protein: 48
Carbs: 26
Fat: 37
Fiber: 2.6

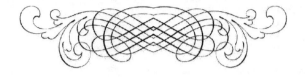

Mongolian Beef (Slow Cooked)

Serves: 4-6

Prep time: 1 minute
Cook time: 8-10 hours
Sauce time: 5 minutes
Total time: 8 hours, 6 minutes – 10 hours, 6 minutes

It's amazing how addicting certain ingredients are when they come together. The sauce for this Mongolian beef is one of those combos. Soy sauce, water, brown sugar, garlic, and ginger serve as the base for chuck roast. The whole thing cooks for 8-1o hours. Serve with rice and scallions on top, for a pop of brightness.

Ingredients:

2 pounds chuck roast
½ cup soy sauce
½ cup brown sugar
¼ cup water
4 minced garlic cloves
½ teaspoon ground ginger
2 tablespoons cornstarch
4 sliced scallions
4-6 cups cooked rice

Instructions:

1. Put beef, soy sauce, water, brown sugar, garlic, and ginger into your Crock-Pot.
2. Stir and close the lid.
3. Cook on SLOW COOK on the low setting for 8-1o hours.

4. When time is up, break up the meat a bit and plate, tenting with foil.
5. To thicken sauce, scoop out ½ cup of cooking liquid.
6. Mix in cornstarch until smooth.
7. Pour back into the Crock-Pot, turning on the BROWN/SAUTÉ setting.
8. Whisk until sauce thickens to your liking.
9. Serve meat and sauce with rice and scallions on top!

Nutritional Info (¼ recipe):
Total calories: 521
Protein: 48
Carbs: 57
Fat: 8
Fiber: 0

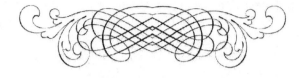

Beef Stroganoff (Pressure Cooked)

<u>*Serves:*</u> 4

Prep time: 10 minutes
Cook time: 8 minutes
Natural pressure releases: 5 minutes
Total time: 23 minutes

Beef stroganoff usually takes a long time, but you can speed up the process using the Multi-Cooker's pressure cooking setting without sacrificing flavor. You brown beef, garlic, and onion together, and then season well with a simple blend of paprika, salt, and pepper. The sauce ingredients go in next, and it cooks for just 8 minutes. Cook noodles separately, because they only take five minutes or so. Wait for a natural pressure release, and then serve with sour cream.

Ingredients:

Glug of extra-virgin olive oil
1 pound ground beef
1 diced onion
3 minced garlic cloves
1 teaspoon paprika
Salt to taste
Black pepper to taste
1 tablespoon flour
1 (10.5-ounce) can of cream of mushroom soup
3 cups beef stock
3 cups dry egg noodles
1 cup sour cream

Instructions:

1. Pour olive oil into your Crock-Pot and hit BROWN/SAUTÉ.
2. When hot, add ground beef, onion, and garlic.
3. Stir to brown.
4. When no longer pink, season well with paprika, salt, and pepper.
5. Turn off the cooker.
6. Stir in flour.
7. Pour in soup and stock.
8. Seal the lid.
9. Hit BEANS/CHILI and adjust time to 8 minutes on high pressure.
10. While that cooks, follow the package instructions for cooking the egg noodles.
11. When time is up, wait 5 minutes, and then quick-release.
12. Make sure beef is 160-degrees, and stir everything together.
13. Serve with sour cream!

Nutritional Info (¼ recipe):
Total calories: 505
Protein: 33
Carbs: 33
Fat: 27
Fiber: 0

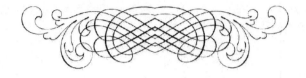

Sesame-Ginger Short Ribs (Slow Cooked)

<u>*Serves:*</u> 8

Prep time: 5 minutes
Cook time: 7-8 hours
Sauce time: 10 minutes
Total time: 7 hours, 15 minutes – 8 hours, 15 minutes

Short ribs are a common sight at Korean BBQs, and are one of my favorite ways to prepare beef. In the Crock-Pot, they take 7-8 hours on the slow cooker setting, and become fall-off-the-bone tender. The sauce is the best combination of salty, sweet, and savory, with ingredients like soy sauce, brown sugar, ginger, and sesame oil. Serve ribs with rice!

<u>Ingredients:</u>

½ cup soy sauce
½ cup beef stock
¼ cup brown sugar
4 minced garlic cloves
½ teaspoon ground ginger
1 teaspoon sesame oil
1 teaspoon crushed red pepper flakes
1 teaspoon dried parsley
5 pounds bone-in short ribs
2 tablespoons cornstarch
6 cups cooked rice

Instructions:

1. In a bowl, mix soy sauce, stock, sugar, garlic, ginger, sesame oil, red pepper flakes, and dried parsley.
2. Grease your Crock-Pot or insert a liner.
3. Cut your short ribs crosswise into bite-sized pieces.
4. Put in the pot, and pour over the sauce.
5. Close the lid.
6. Cook on SLOW COOK, on the low setting, for 7-8 hours.
7. When time is up, ribs should be tender and pulling off the bone.
8. To thicken sauce, scoop out ½ cup of the cooking liquid.
9. Mix in cornstarch until smooth.
10. Hit BROWN/SAUTÉ on your Crock-Pot, and pour in cornstarch mixture.
11. Cook until sauce thickens to your liking.
12. Serve with rice!

Nutritional Info (⅛ recipe):
Total calories: 805
Protein: 54
Carbs: 33
Fat: 50
Fiber: 0

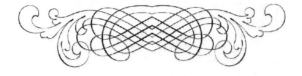

Paprika-Chili Beef Brisket (Slow Cooked)

<u>*Serves:*</u> 4

Prep time: 5 minutes
Cook time: 3-4 hours
Sauce time: 10 minutes
Total time: 3 hours, 15 minutes – 4 hours, 15 minutes

Beef brisket is classic Texas BBQ. For the best eats, you want to slow cook the brisket for 3-4 hours. It cooks in both beef stock and wine, for extra richness, and is seasoned generously with salt, paprika, and chili powder. I like my brisket with a little heat. To make gravy for the meat, simply mix cornstarch into the cooking liquid and simmer to thicken.

Ingredients:

2 pounds beef brisket
1 ⅓ cups beef stock
¼ cup red wine
1 cup diced onion
5 minced garlic cloves
2 teaspoons sea salt
1 teaspoon paprika
1 tablespoon chili powder
¼ cup cold water
2 tablespoons cornstarch

Instructions:

1. Grease your Crock-Pot or insert a liner.
2. Add brisket.
3. Pour in stock and wine.
4. Add garlic and onion around the brisket.
5. Season evenly with salt, paprika, and chili powder.
6. Close the lid.
7. Hit SLOW COOK and cook on LOW for 3-4 hours, until beef is 145-degrees at its thickest part.
8. Remove brisket to rest.
9. While that rests, scoop out ½ cup of the cooking liquid and mix with water.
10. Whisk in cornstarch until smooth.
11. Hit SAUTÉ/BROWN on your Crock-Pot, and whisk in the cornstarch mixture to thicken.
12. Serve brisket with gravy!

Nutritional Info (¼ recipe):
Total calories: 656
Protein: 41
Carbs: 6
Fat: 50
Fiber: 0

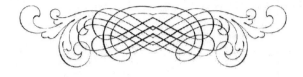

Salisbury Steak (Pressure Cooked)

Serves: 6-8

Prep time: 15 minutes
Cook time: 12 minutes
Gravy time: 6 minutes
Total time: 33 minutes

A TV dinner favorite gets an upgrade using the pressure cooker setting on the Multi-Cooker. You make the "steak" with ground beef, panko, egg, and seasonings like onion powder and garlic. This gets a good browning, along with mushrooms and onion. Cook in stock and balsamic vinegar for 12 minutes. To make the gravy, just thicken the cooking liquid with a cornstarch slurry.

Ingredients:

2 pounds ground beef
⅓ cup Panko bread crumbs
1 egg
1 teaspoon black pepper
½ teaspoon onion powder
½ teaspoon garlic powder
½ teaspoon salt
1 teaspoon Italian seasoning
2 tablespoons extra-virgin olive oil
1 sliced onion
1 pound stemmed and sliced mushrooms
2 cups beef stock
1 tablespoon balsamic vinegar
2 tablespoons cold water
1 tablespoon cornstarch

Instructions:

1. In a bowl, mix ground beef, bread crumbs, egg, and dry seasonings.
2. With your hands, form meat into six to eight patties.

3. Hit BROWN/SAUTÉ on your Crock-Pot and add oil.
4. When hot, brown the patties on both sides.
5. Plate patties for now.
6. Add onion to the hot pot, and cook until turning golden brown.
7. Add mushrooms and cook for another minute or so.
8. Put in patties, and pour over beef stock and balsamic vinegar.
9. Seal the lid.
10. Hit BEANS/CHILI and adjust time to 12 minutes.
11. When time is up, turn off cooker and quick-release the pressure.
12. Ground beef should be cooked to 160-degrees.
13. Take out the patties, onions, and mushrooms, and plate for now.
14. To make gravy, hit BROWN/SAUTÉ again.
15. In a bowl, mix water and cornstarch until smooth.
16. Pour into the Crock-Pot, and stir to thicken.
17. Serve steaks with gravy!

Nutritional Info (⅙ recipe):
Total calories: 323
Protein: 37
Carbs: 8
Fat: 17
Fiber: 1

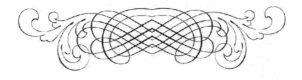

Weeknight Steak 'n Potatoes (Slow Cooked)

<u>*Serves:*</u> 6

Prep time: 12 minutes
Cook time: 7-8 hours
Total time: 7 hours, 12 minutes – 8 hours, 12 minutes

It's the middle of the week, and you don't want to cook when you get home from work or school. Start this meal in the morning, and it'll be ready when you get back. Simply brown seasoned steak in some olive oil, and cook with tomatoes and potatoes for 7-8 hours.

Cooking Note: Steak is cooked to 145-degrees, which is lower than the 160 required for ground beef.

Ingredients:

2 pounds cubed boneless round steak
Salt to taste
Black pepper to taste
3 tablespoons flour
1 tablespoon extra-virgin olive oil
1 large chopped onion
1 (14.5-ounce) can of Italian-style diced tomatoes
1 pound cubed Yukon Gold potatoes

Instructions:

1. Grease your Crock-Pot or insert liner.
2. Season beef with salt, pepper, and flour.
3. Pour oil into a skillet and heat.
4. Add beef and stir to brown all over.

5. Put onions, tomatoes, browned beef, and potatoes in the Crock-Pot.
6. Hit SLOW COOK and cook on the low setting for 7-8 hours.
7. When time is up, make sure beef is 145-degrees.
8. Serve!

Nutritional Info (⅙ recipe):
Total calories: 356
Protein: 36
Carbs: 23
Fat: 14
Fiber: 2.8

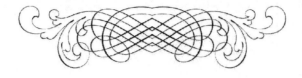

Beef-Potato Hash (Pressure Cooked)

Serves: 6

Prep time: 1 minute
Cook time: 40 minutes
Natural pressure release: 10 minutes
Total time: 51 minutes

An easy, fast meal that uses just 7 ingredients, I love eating leftovers for breakfast. It's a play on the most basic of steak dinners - beef and potatoes. Cook beef stock, onion, garlic, and beef with a tablespoon of Worcestershire for 30 minutes, and then quick-release after 10 minutes. The potatoes go in now, because they take less time to cook, and pressure-cook for another 10 minutes. For freshness, season the finished meal with Italian seasoning.

Ingredients:

1 cup beef stock
1 chopped onion
3 minced garlic cloves
3-pounds boneless chuck roast
1 tablespoon Worcestershire sauce
4 chopped potatoes
Italian seasoning to taste

Instructions:

1. Pour stock, onion, and garlic into your Crock-Pot.
2. Add roast.
3. Pour over Worcestershire sauce.
4. Seal the lid.

5. Hit BEANS/CHILI and adjust time to 30 minutes.
6. When time is up, wait 10 minutes for a natural pressure release, then quick-release leftover pressure.
7. Stir in potatoes and seal the lid again.
8. Hit BEANS/CHILI and cook for another 10 minutes.
9. This time, quick-release the pressure right away when time is up.
10. Season everything with Italian seasoning.
11. Break up meat or shred, and serve!

Nutritional Info (⅙ recipe):
Total calories: 327
Protein: 46
Carbs: 20
Fat: 8
Fiber: 3

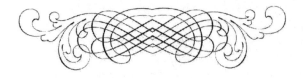

Simple Lamb Curry (Slow Cooked)

Serves: 4

Prep time: 20 minutes
Cook time: 6 hours
Total time: 6 hours, 20 minutes

Curry is one of the most commonly cooked meals in both slow cookers and pressure cookers, so I had to include one recipe for the Multi-Cooker. With easy-to-find ingredients, you don't need to worry about digging through an ethnic market. The only ingredient that might be unique to you is curry paste. The heat is smoothed by coconut milk, which cooks with the cubed, seasoned lamb and cold water for 6 hours on low heat.

Cooking Note: There are yellow, red, and green pastes, with yellow being the mildest one. The paste adds spiciness and flavors like ginger and garlic.

Ingredients:

¼ cup flour
1 ½ pounds cubed lamb shoulder
Salt to taste
Black pepper to taste
2 tablespoons extra-virgin olive oil
1 chopped onion
2 minced garlic cloves
¼ cup curry paste
1 cup lite coconut milk
¾ cup cold water
1 cinnamon stick
4 cups cooked rice

Instructions:

1. Put flour, lamb, salt, and pepper in a Ziploc bag.
2. Shake well until lamb is coated.
3. Hit BROWN/SAUTÉ on your Crock-Pot and add oil.
4. When hot, brown the lamb all over.
5. Remove lamb for now.
6. Add onion and garlic to the hot pan.
7. Cook for 5 minutes, stirring.
8. Add curry paste, stirring for 1 minute.
9. Pour in coconut milk and cold water.
10. When boiling, toss in cinnamon stick, and return lamb to the Crock-Pot.
11. Close the lid.
12. Hit SLOW COOK and cook on the low setting for 6 hours.
13. Pick out the cinnamon stick.
14. Serve lamb curry with rice!

Nutritional Info (¼ recipe):

Total calories: 708
Protein: 52
Carbs: 50
Fat: 33
Fiber: 0

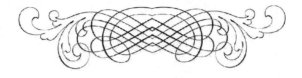

Garlic Lamb Shanks (Pressure Cooked)

<u>*Serves:*</u> 4

Prep time: 12 minutes
Cook time: 30 minutes
Natural pressure release: 10 minutes
Sauce time: 10 minutes
Total time: 1 hour, 2 minutes

I love serving lamb shanks for holidays, because they seem more special than beef. Lamb might seem intimidating if you haven't cooked it a lot, but it cooks a lot like steak, and the pressure cooker setting ensures it's never tough. After browning seasoned lamb, it cooks in a mixture of chicken stock, wine, tomato paste, and thyme for 30 minutes. After a natural pressure release, you add butter and balsamic vinegar to the cooking liquid, which becomes sauce!

<u>*Ingredients:*</u>

2-pounds lamb shanks
Salt to taste
Black pepper to taste
1 tablespoon extra-virgin olive oil
8 chopped garlic cloves
1 cup chicken stock
1 cup red wine
2 tablespoons tomato paste
1 teaspoon dried thyme
1 tablespoon butter
1 teaspoon balsamic vinegar

Instructions:

1. Season lamb well with salt and pepper.
2. Turn your Crock-Pot to BROWN/SAUTÉ and add oil.
3. When hot, add lamb and brown on both sides.
4. Plate for now.
5. Add garlic to the hot pot and cook until turning golden.
6. Pour in stock, wine, tomato paste, and dried thyme.
7. When tomato paste has dissolved, return the lamb and seal the lid.
8. Hit BEANS/CHILI and adjust time to 30 minutes on high pressure.
9. When time is up, wait for a natural pressure release.
10. When pressure is gone, take out the lamb and tent with foil.
11. Hit BROWN/SAUTÉ again and bring cooking liquid to a boil for 5 minutes.
12. Add in butter and vinegar, and turn off the Crock-Pot.
13. Serve lamb with plenty of sauce!

Nutritional Info (¼ recipe):

Total calories: 543
Protein: 34
Carbs: 16
Fat: 34
Fiber: 0

Chapter 6: Poultry

If I had to name the most versatile meat, I would have to say chicken. It has a mild flavor, so it goes with just about every other flavor. There are breasts, thighs, and wings, and you can make both casual and fancy meals with it. This section explores all the different ways you can prepare chicken (and turkey) using the Multi-Cooker. You'll be slow cooking meals like butter chicken, an Indian classic, and pressure cooking turkey breast and gravy, for when you feel like Thanksgiving dinner free of the hassle of long cooking times. If you're in a rut when it comes to poultry, these recipes will break you out of it.

Teriyaki Chicken Sandwiches (Pressure Cooked) 66
Butter Chicken (Slow Cooked) 68
Chicken 'n Dumplings (Slow Cooked) 70
Hawaiian BBQ Chicken (Pressure Cooked) 72
Chicken Cordon Bleu (Slow Cooked) 74
Easy Buffalo Chicken (Slow Cooked) 76
Salsa Verde Turkey + Rice (Pressure Cooked) 78
Turkey Breast w/ Gravy (Pressure Cooked) 80
Dijon Turkey + Gravy (Pressure Cooked) 82
Thanksgiving Turkey (Slow Cooked) 84

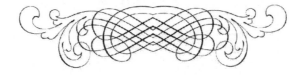

Teriyaki Chicken Sandwiches (Pressure Cooked)

<u>Serves:</u> 6-8

Prep time: 5 minutes
Cook time: 12 minutes
Total time: 17 minutes

With just six total ingredients, this recipe for chicken sandwiches is ideal for really busy nights when you need to eat and run. Prep time is just 5 minutes, and cook time is only 12. You whisk honey and bottled teriyaki sauce into the Multi-Cooker, add chicken stock, and then add chicken. After a quick-release, use a fork to shred the meat, and pile onto hamburgers buns with a crisp lettuce leaf. That's it!

<u>**Ingredients:**</u>

1 tablespoon honey
⅔ cup teriyaki sauce
¼ cup chicken stock
2 pounds chicken breasts
6-8 lettuce leaves
6-8 hamburger buns

<u>**Instructions:**</u>

1. Whisk honey and teriyaki into your Crock-Pot.
2. Pour in chicken stock.
3. Add breasts, turning to coat.
4. Seal the lid.

5. Hit BEANS/CHILI and adjust time to 12 minutes on high pressure.
6. When time is up, quick-release the pressure.
7. Shred the chicken.
8. Divide chicken and lettuce evenly on hamburger buns to serve!

Nutritional Info (⅙ recipe):
Total calories: 196
Protein: 13
Carbs: 30
Fat: 2
Fiber: 0

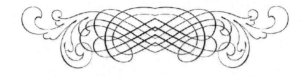

Butter Chicken (Slow Cooked)

<u>*Serves:*</u> 6

Prep time: 30 minutes
Cook time: 6-8 hours
Total time: 6 hours, 30 minutes – 8 hours, 30 minutes

Butter chicken is one of the most popular Indian dishes both there and in the United States. It's accessible and uses easy-to-get ingredients like yogurt, tomato paste, and coconut milk. The only ingredients you may not have used are curry powder and garam masala, a fragrant spice that includes cinnamon, cumin, and cloves. They're available at any grocery store. For really tender chicken thighs, slow cook for 6-8 hours.

<u>*Ingredients:*</u>

2 tablespoons extra-virgin olive oil
2 tablespoons butter
4 chopped skinless + boneless chicken thighs
1 diced onion
3 minced garlic cloves
1 tablespoon curry powder
1 teaspoon garam masala
6-ounces tomato paste
1 cup plain yogurt
1 (14-ounce) can of coconut milk
½ teaspoon ground cinnamon
½ teaspoon ground nutmeg
¼ teaspoon ground cloves
Pinch of salt

Instructions:

1. Heat butter and oil in a skillet until melted.
2. Mix in chicken, onion, and garlic, and cook until the onion is clear.
3. Stir in curry powder, garam masala, and tomato paste until smooth.
4. Pour mixture into a greased Crock-Pot.
5. Stir in yogurt, coconut milk, and spices, including salt.
6. Close the lid.
7. Hit SLOW COOK and cook on the low setting for 6-8 hours.
8. Chicken should be at least 165-degrees.
9. Serve chicken with lots of sauce!

Nutritional Info (⅙ recipe):
Total calories: 288
Protein: 22
Carbs: 11
Fat: 18
Fiber: 0

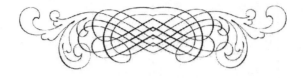

Chicken 'n Dumplings (Slow Cooked)

Serves: 8

Prep time: 1 minute
Cook time: 5 hours, 10 minutes
Total time: 5 hours, 11 minutes

When the weather gets cold, that means it's comfort food season. This slow-cooked chicken 'n dumplings recipe is semi-homemade for your convenience, and serves up to 8 people. Cover chicken, butter, cream of chicken soup, and an onion in water, and cook for 4 hours on high temperature. Now, you'll add the biscuit dough, because it cooks faster. Simply roll out the biscuits and cut into strips. Throw in some frozen peas now, too, while you're at it. Cook for another hour, shred chicken, and then finish cooking for just 10 minutes.

Ingredients:

4 skinless + boneless chicken breasts
2 tablespoons butter
2 (10.75-ounce) cans cream of chicken soup
1 diced onion
Enough water to cover the ingredients
1 (8-piece) can of buttermilk biscuit dough
2 cups thawed frozen peas

Instructions:

1. Grease your Crock-Pot or insert a liner.
2. Add chicken, butter, soup, and onion.
3. Pour in enough water to cover the ingredients.
4. Cook on SLOW COOK for 5 hours on the high setting.

5. When there's an hour left, roll out the biscuits and cut into strips.
6. Add peas to Crock-Pot, and lay biscuit strips on top.
7. Close the lid again and cook for the rest of the time.
8. When time is up, you can shred the chicken.
9. Cook for another 10 minutes, to finish up the biscuits, and serve!

Nutritional Info (⅛ recipe):
Total calories: 290
Protein: 19
Carbs: 26
Fat: 13
Fiber: 2

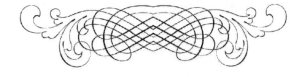

Hawaiian BBQ Chicken (Pressure Cooked)

Serves: 4

Prep time: 10 minutes
Cook time: 5 minutes
Simmer time: 5 minutes
Total time: 20 minutes

BBQ chicken is a summertime favorite around my house, and my daughter especially loves this Hawaiian BBQ. Sweetened with pineapple chunks and juice, chopped and browned chicken cooks for 5 minutes under pressure with BBQ sauce and seasonings. To thicken the sauce, you add cornstarch slurry after a quick-release, and simmer until thickened. You'll have to resist licking the sauce off if it gets on your fingers. Serve chicken as is, on top of salad, or as a sandwich.

Ingredients:

4 chopped boneless + skinless chicken breasts
Salt to taste
Black pepper to taste
Garlic powder to taste
1 tablespoon extra-virgin olive oil
1 cup BBQ sauce (your choice)
1 (8-ounce) can pineapple chunks (keep juice)
2 tablespoons cold water
2 tablespoons cornstarch

Instructions:

1. Season chicken with salt, pepper, and garlic powder.
2. Turn your Crock-Pot to BROWN/SAUTÉ and add oil.

3. Cook chicken, stirring every now and then, so cooking is even.
4. When chicken is golden, turn off the cooker.
5. Add ½ cup BBQ sauce and pineapple *juice*.
6. Seal the lid.
7. Hit BEANS/CHILI and adjust time to just 5 minutes on high pressure.
8. When time is up, quick-release the pressure.
9. Make sure chicken is 165-degrees.
10. In a bowl, mix water and cornstarch until smooth.
11. Pour into your Crock-Pot, and hit BROWN/SAUTÉ again.
12. Simmer to let sauce thicken.
13. Pour in the rest of the BBQ sauce and pineapple chunks.
14. Stir and serve!

Nutritional Info (¼ recipe):
Total calories: 247
Protein: 26
Carbs: 12
Fat: 7
Fiber: 0

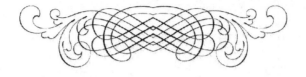

Chicken Cordon Bleu (Slow Cooked)

Serves: 6

Prep time: 5 minutes
Cook time: 4-6 hours
Total time: 4 hours, 5 minutes – 6 hours, 5 minutes

Traditionally a fancy French dish, this version is much easier and doesn't involve stuffing chicken breasts with anything. There's a bit of layering involved - coat bottom of your Crock-Pot with milk and cream of chicken soup, add halved chicken breasts, then ham and Swiss cheese, and then the rest of the sauce. That cooks on low for 4-6 hours.

Ingredients:

1 (10.75-ounce) can of cream of chicken soup
1 cup milk
6 skinless and boneless chicken breasts
6 slices ham
6 Swiss cheese slices

Instructions:

1. In a bowl, mix cream of chicken soup and milk.
2. Pour into a greased Crock-Pot, just enough to coat the bottom.
3. Cut your chicken breasts in half.
4. Put in the cooker.
5. Cover with ham and cheese.
6. Pour the rest of the sauce on top.
7. Close the lid.
8. Press SLOW COOK and cook on low for 4-6 hours, until chicken is 165-degrees.

9. Serve!

Nutritional Info (⅙ recipe):
Total calories: 333
Protein: 40
Carbs: 9
Fat: 16
Fiber: 0

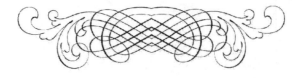

Easy Buffalo Chicken (Slow Cooked)

<u>*Serves:*</u> 6

Prep time: 1 minute
Cook time: 7-9 hours
Total time: 7 hours, 1 minute – 9 hours, 1 minute

Buffalo chicken has a really unique flavor, so instead of trying to make your own right now, this recipe calls for bottled Buffalo wing sauce. Coat chicken in this sauce in the Crock-Pot, and sprinkle on spices like dried parsley and chives. This cooks for 7-9 hours on low temperature. Butter goes in last, and cooks for another hour before it's ready to serve.

<u>*Ingredients:*</u>

3 pounds boneless + skinless chicken breasts
12-ounces Buffalo wing sauce
1 tablespoon dried parsley
1 teaspoon dried chives
1 teaspoon onion powder
1 teaspoon garlic powder
2 tablespoons butter

<u>*Instructions:*</u>

1. Grease your Crock-Pot well or insert liner.
2. Add chicken breasts and pour over wing sauce.
3. Add in dry spices.
4. Cook on SLOW COOK for 7-9 hours on LOW.
5. Shred chicken.
6. Add butter and stir until melted.
7. Close the lid and cook on SLOW COOK again for 1 hour on the

low setting.
8. Serve!

Nutritional Info (⅙ recipe):
Total calories: 414
Protein: 69
Carbs: 0
Fat: 13
Fiber: 0

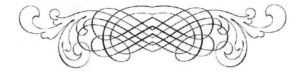

Salsa Verde Turkey + Rice (Pressure Cooked)

Serves: 6-8

Prep time: 1 minute
Cook time: 18 minutes
Natural pressure release: 15 minutes
Total time: 34 minutes

I love using salsa as an ingredient in cooking, because it brings so much flavor. No need to bother with a bunch of dry spices. This one-pot meal has you pour rice and chicken stock into the Crock-Pot, and pile on onion, turkey tenderloin, salsa verde, and a little garlic and salt on top. Cook for 18 minutes on the pressure cooker setting and then allow the pressure to come down on its own. Serve!

Ingredients:

2 ½ cups chicken stock
2 cups long-grain brown rice
1 diced onion
2 pounds turkey tenderloins
1 cup salsa verde
1 teaspoon garlic powder
Healthy pinch of salt

Instructions:

1. Add chicken stock and rice to your Crock-Pot.
2. Add the rest of the ingredients on top - don't stir them in.
3. Seal the lid.

4. Hit BEANS/CHILI and cook for 18 minutes on high pressure.
5. When time is up, wait for a natural pressure release.
6. When the pressure is gone, the meal is ready!

Nutritional Info (⅙ recipe):
Total calories: 397
Protein: 44
Carbs: 51
Fat: 3
Fiber: 2.6

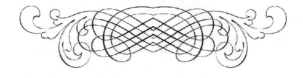

Turkey Breast w/ Gravy (Pressure Cooked)

Serves: 8

Prep time: 1 minute
Cook time: 30 minutes
Natural pressure release: 10 minutes
Simmer time: 5 minutes
Total time: 46 minutes

Sometimes you don't want to serve a whole turkey for Thanksgiving. This recipe for just the breast serves 8, and is seasoned with classic ingredients like salt, pepper, Italian seasoning, onion, and garlic. It even makes its own gravy. The turkey breast should go on top of a trivet in the cooker, so it doesn't scorch. When it's done cooking (in 30 minutes), remove turkey, and make the gravy by mixing in a cornstarch slurry and simmering.

Ingredients:

6 ½-pound bone-in, skin-on turkey breast
Salt to taste
Black pepper to taste
Italian seasoning to taste (salt-free)
1 ¾ cups chicken stock
1 sliced onion
3 whole garlic cloves
3 tablespoons cold water
3 tablespoons cornstarch

Instructions:

1. Season your turkey breast with salt, pepper, and Italian seasoning.
2. Lower trivet into your Crock-Pot - you don't want the breast touching the bottom directly.
3. Pour in stock, and add onion and garlic.
4. Put turkey on the trivet and seal the lid.
5. Hit BEANS/CHILI and adjust time to 30 minutes on high pressure.
6. When time is up, wait for a natural pressure release.
7. Turkey should be at least 165-degrees at its thickest part.
8. Plate turkey.
9. Remove garlic and onion from the pot, and skim excess fat from the top.
10. In a bowl, mix water and cornstarch.
11. Add to the Crock-Pot and hit BROWN/SAUTÉ.
12. Simmer to let gravy thicken.
13. Serve slices of turkey breast with gravy!

Nutritional Info (⅛ recipe):
Total calories: 412
Protein: 67
Carbs: 5
Fat: 12
Fiber: 0

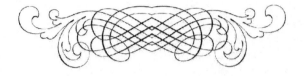

Dijon Turkey + Gravy (Pressure Cooked)

<u>*Serves:*</u> 4-6

Prep time: 12 minutes
Cook time: 30 minutes
Simmer time: 5 minutes
Total time: 47 minutes

Want to use up that big bag of turkey thighs and breasts you have? This recipe takes less than an hour, and flavors the turkey with garlic, white wine, and Italian seasoning. Browning the turkey ensures better flavor, too. When the turkey is done, you use the cooking liquid to make the gravy, which is flavored with Dijon mustard and thickened with cornstarch.

Cooking Note: Deglazing is when you pour a liquid in the pot, and scraping up stuck-on food bits. Those brown bits add tons of flavor.

Ingredients:

3 pounds bone-in turkey thighs + breasts
Salt to taste
Black pepper to taste
1 tablespoon extra-virgin olive oil
2 sliced onions
3 peeled whole garlic cloves
½ cup chicken stock
½ cup white wine
2 tablespoons Dijon mustard
1 teaspoon Italian seasoning
2 tablespoons cold water
1 tablespoon flour

Instructions:

1. Season turkey with salt and pepper.
2. Turn your Crock-Pot to BROWN/SAUTÉ and add oil.
3. Sear the turkey on three minutes per side, until evenly brown.
4. Plate turkey for now, leaving the Crock-Pot on.
5. Add onions and garlic to the pot, and cook for 5 minutes or so.
6. Pour in wine and broth, deglazing the pot.
7. Stir in mustard and Italian seasoning.
8. Return turkey to the pot and seal the lid.
9. Hit BEANS/CHILI and adjust time to 30 minutes on high pressure.
10. When time is up, wait for a natural pressure release.
11. Plate the turkey.
12. To make the gravy, begin by pureeing the cooking liquid until smooth. You can use an immersion blender or regular blender. Return to Crock-Pot.
13. Mix water and flour in a bowl until smooth.
14. Pour into the gravy and hit BROWN/SAUTÉ.
15. Simmer until thickened.
16. Serve with turkey!

Nutritional Info (¼ recipe):
Total calories: 525
Protein: 89
Carbs: 8
Fat: 24
Fiber: 0

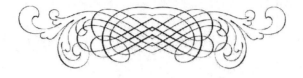

Thanksgiving Turkey (Slow Cooked)

Serves: 10

Prep time: 7 minutes
Cook time: 8 hours
Broil time: 10 minutes
Total time: 8 hours, 17 minutes

It's Thanksgiving time and that means time to make a turkey! To free up the oven, how about making your turkey in the Multi-Cooker this year? It's seasoned with a simple compound butter with Italian seasoning, garlic, salt, and pepper. Slow cook on the low temperature setting for 8 hours. To get a nice, crispy skin, you rub on more butter and broil for just 10 minutes.

Ingredients:

4 tablespoons butter
1 teaspoon Italian seasoning
1 teaspoon garlic powder
Salt to taste
Black pepper to taste
8-pound skin-on whole turkey
6 peeled whole garlic cloves
Bundle of fresh herbs (your choice)

Instructions:

1. Mix butter, Italian seasoning, garlic powder, and salt.
2. Put half in the fridge.
3. Grease your Crock-Pot and put in the garlic.
4. Add herbs.
5. Dry the turkey with paper towels and rub with the herb butter you

left out of the fridge.
6. Sprinkle on more salt and pepper.
7. Put turkey in your Crock-Pot and close the lid.
8. Cook on SLOW COOK for 8 hours on LOW.
9. When time is up, carefully remove the turkey and stick in a roasting pan.
10. If you're planning on using the cooking liquid as gravy, scoop out 2 cups from the Crock-Pot. Pour the rest over the turkey.
11. Take out the refrigerated herb butter, and slather all over the top of the turkey.
12. Broil turkey for 1o minutes to get a crispy skin.
13. Rest for a few minute and serve!

Nutritional Info (1/10 recipe):
Total calories: 587
Protein: 67
Carbs: 1
Fat: 33
Fiber: 0

Chapter 7: Pork

Pork is sometimes a difficult meat to master, because it has the tendency to dry out. With the Multi-Cooker, it's easy to cook for the perfect amount of time, whether you're slow cooking or pressure cooking. This section has recipes for every cut of pork, including pork chops, roasts, and ribs. There's even a recipe for pork belly for people who've never made it. Pork belly is one of my favorite things to make; it's basically bacon at its best. There's also a glazed ham recipe that's perfect for Christmas, Easter, or any other large gathering.

Honey-Ginger Pork Chops (Slow Cooked) *88*
Honey-Mustard Pork Chops (Pressure Cooked) *90*
Pork Roast w/ Maple Gravy (Slow Cooked) *92*
Pork Carnitas (Slow Cooked) *94*
Blackberry-Cider Pork Loin (Pressure Cooked) *96*
Coconut Milk-Braised Pork (Slow Cooked) *98*
One-Pot Pork Chop Meal (Pressure Cooked) *100*
Dr. Pepper Baby Back Ribs (Slow Cooked) *102*
Beginner's Pork Belly (Pressure Cooked) *104*
Classic Glazed Ham (Pressure Cooked) *106*

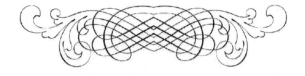

Honey-Ginger Pork Chops (Slow Cooked)

Serves: 4

Prep time: 7 minutes
Cook time: 4-5 hours
Gravy time: 2 minutes
Total time: 4 hours, 9 minutes – 5 hours, 9 minutes

Pork has a naturally slightly-sweet flavor, which means it pairs really well with other sweet ingredients like honey. To cut through that, this recipe uses paprika, garlic powder, and fresh ginger! To get a nice crust on the pork, brown for a total of 6 minutes before cooking for 4-5 hours. To make a gravy, simply mix cornstarch into the cooking liquid.

Ingredients:

4 pork chops
1 teaspoon paprika
1 teaspoon garlic powder
Salt to taste
Glug of extra-virgin olive oil
½ cup honey
2 tablespoons soy sauce
One lime's worth of juice
1-inch peeled and sliced thumb of ginger
1 tablespoon cold water
2 tablespoons cornstarch

Instructions:

1. Season chops with paprika, garlic powder, and salt.
2. Heat olive oil in a skillet, and add pork.

3. Sear until golden, which takes about 3 minutes per side.
4. In a bowl, mix the honey, soy sauce, lime juice, and sliced ginger.
5. Grease the Crock-Pot and add pork.
6. Pour the sauce over and close the lid.
7. Hit SLOW COOK and cook on low for 4-5 hours, until pork is 145-degrees.
8. To make sauce, mix water and cornstarch in a cup.
9. Plate the pork, and pour water/cornstarch mixture into the Crock-Pot.
10. Stir until thickened.
11. Serve pork with gravy!

Nutritional Info (¼ recipe):
Total calories: 425
Protein: 28
Carbs: 39
Fat: 18
Fiber: 0

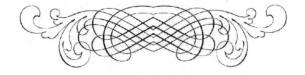

Honey-Mustard Pork Chops (Pressure Cooked)

Serves: 4

Prep time: 10 minutes
Cook time: 8 minutes
Natural pressure release: 10 minutes
Gravy time: 5 minutes
Total time: 33 minutes

Honey-mustard is a classic pork accompaniment, and it's so easy to make: just mix Dijon and honey together! After browning the chops, you pour in the honey mustard along with chicken stock and a little salt. Pressure cook for just 8 minutes and wait for a natural pressure release. Mix in cornstarch slurry to thicken up the sauce.

Ingredients:

4 bone-in pork chops
1 tablespoon extra-virgin olive oil
3 minced garlic cloves
1 small minced onion
2 cups chicken stock
½ cup Dijon mustard
¼ cup honey
Salt to taste
2 tablespoons cold water
2 tablespoons cornstarch

Instructions:

1. Hit BROWN/SAUTÉ on your Crock-Pot and heat oil.
2. When hot, brown the pork chops on both sides, about 3 minutes per side.
3. Plate for now.
4. Add garlic and onion, and cook for a few minutes, until no longer raw.
5. In a bowl, mix chicken stock, mustard, honey, and salt.
6. Return pork chops to the Crock-Pot, and pour over the liquid.
7. Seal the lid.
8. Hit BEANS/CHILI and cook on high pressure for 8 minutes.
9. When time is up, wait for a natural pressure release.
10. Make sure pork is 145-degrees at its thickest part.
11. If pork is done, remove and plate.
12. Turn the Crock-Pot to BROWN/SAUTÉ again.
13. Mix water and cornstarch together in a cup, and pour into the pot, whisking to thicken.
14. Serve pork chops with gravy!

Nutritional Info (¼ recipe):
Total calories: 358
Protein: 29
Carbs: 21
Fat: 18
Fiber: 0

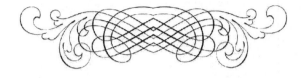

Pork Roast w/ Maple Gravy (Slow Cooked)

Serves: 4

Prep time: 3 minutes
Cook time: 7-9 hours
Gravy time: 5 minutes
Total time: 7 hours, 8 minutes – 9 hours, 8 minutes

Pork roasts were made for slow cookers. They become the perfect texture and still juicy. The pork is seasoned with just salt, and then cooked in chicken stock, mustard, maple syrup, balsamic vinegar, and Italian seasoning. After 7-9 hours, the pork should be ready. Thicken gravy with cornstarch slurry.

Ingredients:

2-pound pork roast
Salt to taste
2 tablespoons chicken stock
2 tablespoons Dijon mustard
2 tablespoons pure maple syrup
1 tablespoon balsamic vinegar
1 teaspoon Italian seasoning
1 tablespoon cold water
1 tablespoon cornstarch

Instructions:

1. Season pork well with salt.
2. Grease your Crock-Pot and put in pork.
3. In a bowl, mix chicken stock, mustard, maple syrup, balsamic vinegar, and Italian seasoning.

4. Pour over the pork and close the lid.
5. Press SLOW COOK and cook on low for 7-9 hours, until pork is 145-degrees.
6. Take out the pork and tent with foil while finishing the gravy.
7. Mix cornstarch and water in a cup.
8. Spoon out some of the cooking liquid and mix in your cornstarch mixture until smooth.
9. Hit SAUTÉ/BROWN on your Crock-Pot and pour in slurry.
10. Stir until thickened to your liking.
11. Serve pork with gravy!

Nutritional Info (¼ recipe):
Total calories: 598
Protein: 61
Carbs: 8
Fat: 33
Fiber: 0

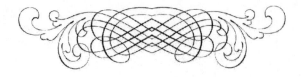

Pork Carnitas (Slow Cooked)

Serves: 10-12

Prep time: 3 minutes
Cook time: 8-10 hours
Reduction time: 10 minutes
Crisp time: 15 minutes
Total time: 8 hours, 28 minutes – 10 hours, 28 minutes

Pork carnitas made from bone-in pork shoulder is one of the best uses for your Multi-Cooker. Cooked low and slow, the pork practically falls apart by itself when it's done. For a variety of flavors, I like to use a mix of garlic, cumin, oregano, and paprika for spices, as well as a jalapeno and both lime and orange juice. That gives the finished product heat, sweetness, and acidity. To get the pork crispy, it's broiled in the oven for 15 minutes after cooking.

Ingredients:

5 pounds bone-in pork shoulder
1 tablespoon extra-virgin olive oil
1 tablespoon garlic powder
3 teaspoons ground cumin
½ tablespoon dried oregano
1 teaspoon paprika
Salt to taste
Black pepper to taste
1 chopped onion
1 chopped and seeded jalapeno
½ cup orange juice
¼ cup lime juice

Instructions:

1. Pat your pork shoulder dry.
2. Mix olive oil, garlic, cumin, oregano, paprika, salt, and pepper together in a bowl.
3. Rub all over the pork shoulder.
4. Grease your Crock-Pot and put in the shoulder, fatty side up.
5. Add onion, jalapeno, and juices.
6. Cook on SLOW COOK for 8-10 hours on the low setting, until meat is 145-degrees at its thickest part, and falling apart.
7. Remove the pork and cool for a few minutes.
8. Shred.
9. Skim excess fat off the cooking liquid, and reduce to 1 ½ cups on the BROWN/SAUTÉ setting, if necessary.
10. To get crispy pork, put just enough pork to fit in a hot skillet with crowding, and pour in a little reduced cooking liquid.
11. Don't stir the pork - let it get crisp on the one side.
12. When the liquid has evaporated, that batch is done.
13. Keep repeating until all the pork is crisped up.
14. Serve!

Nutritional Info (1/10 recipe):
Total calories: 402
Protein: 30
Carbs: 3
Fat: 28
Fiber: 0

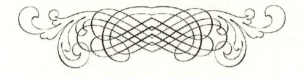

Blackberry-Cider Pork Loin (Pressure Cooked)

<u>Serves:</u> 4

Prep time: 10 minutes
Cook time: 20 minutes
Natural pressure release: 5 minutes
Total time: 35 minutes

For a recipe with just seven total ingredients, this pork loin has a *lot* of flavor. I love using ciders in cooking; it's an easy way to infuse meat with flavor and create a great base for sauces. You use blackberry cider (or pear blackberry, if that's what's available), and cook it with seasoned and browned pork and onion. Cook for 20 minutes, and then wait 5 minutes before quick-releasing.

<u>*Ingredients:*</u>

2 pounds pork tenderloin
Salt to taste
2 teaspoons garlic powder
2 tablespoons onion powder
2 tablespoons olive oil
1 chopped onion
2 cups blackberry cider (like Crispin's Pear Blackberry)

<u>*Instructions:*</u>

1. Season pork loin with salt, garlic powder, and onion powder.
2. Pour olive oil into your Crock-Pot and hit BROWN/SAUTÉ.

3. Sear the pork on both sides, about 3 minutes per side.
4. Plate for now.
5. Add onion and cook until fragrant.
6. Return the pork to the pot and pour in cider.
7. Seal the lid.
8. Hit BEANS/CHILI and adjust time to 20 minutes.
9. When time is up, wait 5 minutes, and then release the pressure.
10. Pork should be 145-degrees at its thickest part.
11. Slice and serve!

Nutritional Info (¼ recipe):
Total calories: 402
Protein: 43
Carbs: 12
Fat: 15
Fiber: 0

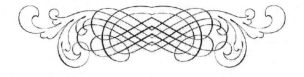

Coconut Milk-Braised Pork (Slow Cooked)

<u>*Serves:*</u> 4-6

Prep time: 15 minutes
Cook time: 8 hours
Total time: 8 hours, 15 minutes

Coconut milk and pork may seem like an odd combination, but the flavors are actually very complimentary. Pork's sweetness has a slightly nutty flavor to me, just like coconut milk. Fish sauce cuts through the richness, while green onions to top off the cooked pork shoulder bring brightness to the meal.

Ingredients:

2 tablespoons extra-virgin olive oil
3 pounds chopped boneless pork shoulder
¼ cup fish sauce
1 ½ cups lite coconut milk
5 chopped green onions

Instructions:

1. Heat a skillet and add olive oil.
2. When the oil is hot, sear pork all over, until a deep golden-brown.
3. Grease your Crock-Pot or insert a liner.
4. Add pork.
5. Pour over fish sauce and coconut milk. You want all but ⅓ of the pork to be covered.
6. Close the lid.
7. Cook on SLOW COOK for 8 hours on low heat.

8. Pork should be 145-degrees.
9. Serve with cooking liquid to moisten, and green onions!

Nutritional Info (¼ recipe):
Total calories: 857
Protein: 59
Carbs: 8
Fat: 66
Fiber: 0

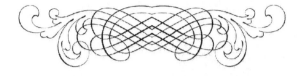

One-Pot Pork Chop Meal (Pressure Cooked)

<u>*Serves:*</u> 4

Prep time: 1 minute
Cook time: 5 minutes
Natural pressure release: 5 minutes
Total time: 11 minutes

Cook pork, rice, and veggies in just one pot, in less than 20 minutes! This is the perfect meal for nights when you really don't feel like cooking. You simply layer all the ingredients in the Crock-Pot, in the order they appear, and cook for only 5 minutes. Let the pressure come down naturally, and it's ready to eat!

Cooking Note: If pork chops don't seem thin enough, pound. You want like stir-fry thin pork.

<u>*Ingredients:*</u>

1 tablespoon extra-virgin olive oil
1 chopped onion
1 cup dry basmati rice (longest-grain you can find)
1 teaspoon salt
1 teaspoon garlic powder
4 thin-cut pork chops
¾ cup chicken stock
½ cup frozen vegetables

<u>*Instructions:*</u>

1. Grease your Crock-Pot well or insert a liner.
2. Layer ingredients in the order they appear in the list.

3. Make sure the rice is completely covered with liquid.
4. Seal the lid.
5. Hit BEANS/CHILI and cook for just 5 minutes on high pressure.
6. Wait for a natural pressure release when the timer beeps.
7. Serve!

Nutritional Info (¼ recipe):
Total calories: 323
Protein: 27
Carbs: 43
Fat: 5
Fiber: 1

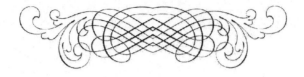

Dr. Pepper Baby Back Ribs (Slow Cooked)

Serves: 6

Prep time: 1 minute
Cook time: 8 hours
Total time: 8 hours, 1 minute

Baby back ribs should always be slow cooked; they become fall-off-the-bone tender. In this recipe, you use Dr. Pepper as your sweet ingredient, with a BBQ sauce of your choice, so you can make that as spicy or mild as you like. I recommend one that isn't sweet, because of the soda. The ribs, which you season with salt, pepper, garlic, and parsley, cook overnight or all day for 8 hours.

Ingredients:

1 rack baby back ribs
Sea salt to taste
Black pepper to taste
Garlic powder to taste
2 teaspoons dried parsley
1 teaspoon Worcestershire sauce
1 cup BBQ sauce (your choice)
1 (12-ounce) can of Dr. Pepper

Instructions:

1. Cut ribs in half, so they fit in your Crock-Pot.
2. Sprinkle dry seasonings evenly over meat.
3. Pour over Worcestershire, BBQ sauce, and soda.
4. Close the lid.
5. Cook on SLOW COOK for 8 hours on the low setting.

6. When time is up, make sure ribs are *at least* 145-degrees, though if they're falling off the bone, they're definitely ready.
7. Enjoy!

Nutritional Info (⅙ recipe):
Total calories: 216
Protein: 21
Carbs: 12
Fat: 11
Fiber: 0

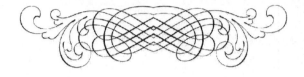

Beginner's Pork Belly (Pressure Cooked)

<u>Serves:</u> 4-6

Prep time: 6 minutes
Cook time: 40 minutes
Natural pressure release: 12 minutes
Sear time: 6 minutes
Rest time: 7 minutes
Total time: 1 hour, 11 minutes

If you know me, you know I love talking about how good pork belly is, and how more people should use it. It's like bacon and steak had a baby. If it's your first time making the meat, the pressure cooking setting on the Multi-Cooker is a great method. Put pork belly in the Crock-Pot with chicken stock, sprinkle in seasonings, and bring to a boil. Then you seal the lid and cook on high. Wait for a natural pressure release.

Cooking Note: This recipe has you cook the pork belly for 40 minutes. If you want it with a texture more like steak, cook for just 30 minutes. An hour will make the pork belly *really* tender, with a braised quality.

<u>Ingredients:</u>

1 pound pork belly
Enough chicken stock to come up ¼ inch in Crock-Pot
Salt to taste
1 teaspoon garlic powder
Italian seasoning to taste
1 tablespoon extra-virgin olive oil

Instructions:

1. Grease your Crock-Pot.
2. Place pork belly inside, and pour in chicken stock. You only need about ¼-inch's worth.
3. Season pork with salt, garlic powder, and Italian seasoning.
4. Hit BROWN/SAUTÉ and wait until the chicken stock begins to boil.
5. Immediately seal the lid, and hit BEANS/CHILI, adjusting time to 40 minutes on high pressure.
6. When time is up, wait for a natural pressure release.
7. To get a golden crust on the pork belly, heat a skillet with olive oil.
8. When it's really hot, add pork and sear 2-3 minutes per side.
9. Rest for 7 minutes or so, then slice and serve!

Nutritional Info (¼ recipe):
Total calories: 620
Protein: 11
Carbs: 0
Fat: 64
Fiber: 0

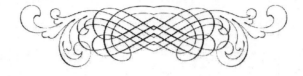

Classic Glazed Ham (Pressure Cooked)

Serves: 10

Prep time: 5 minutes
Cook time: 15 minutes
Natural pressure release: 15 minutes
Oven time: 5-10 minutes
Total time: 40-45 minutes

Ham with a sweet glaze is a favorite for many families, especially during the holidays. Pressure cooking it is a great way to cut down on time in the kitchen. For a cooking liquid, use white wine. The glaze is brown sugar, maple syrup, Dijon, balsamic vinegar, and cloves. Half of it goes on the ham before it's cooked, while the rest of it gets used when you stick the ham in the oven for a final 5-10 minutes.

Ingredients:

6-ounces white wine
¼ cup brown sugar
1 cup pure maple syrup
3 tablespoons Dijon mustard
1 teaspoon balsamic vinegar
1 teaspoon ground cloves
8-pounds ham

Instructions:

1. Pour wine into your Crock-Pot.
2. In a bowl, mix brown sugar, maple syrup, mustard, balsamic vinegar, and ground cloves.
3. Brush ham with half of the glaze.

4. Put in your Crock-Pot, sealing the lid.
5. Cook on BEANS/CHILI for 15 minutes on LOW pressure.
6. When time is up, wait 15 minutes for a natural pressure release. While you wait, preheat oven to 400-degrees.
7. Put ham and any cooking liquid into a baking dish.
8. Brush on the rest of the glaze.
9. Cook ham in the oven until skin turns golden-brown, which should take between 5-10 minutes.
10. Serve!

Nutritional Info (1/10 recipe):
Total calories: 718
Protein: 68
Carbs: 35
Fat: 30
Fiber: 0

Chapter 8: Seafood

Seafood is often a neglected choice for a main dish, because it can be tricky to know what to do with it. This section gives you lots of ideas for a variety of the sea's bounty, including salmon, haddock, shrimp, and even mussels. Just about every flavor and spice has a complimentary seafood, so you'll find dishes that use maple syrup, ginger, Old Bay seasoning, and turmeric. Because seafood cooks so quickly, you'll see some of the shortest cooking times for both the pressure cooking and slow cooking settings on the Multi-Cooker.

Easy Maple Salmon (Slow Cooked) 110
Creamy Haddock + Spinach (Pressure Cooked) 112
Shrimp Boil (Slow Cooked) 114
Shrimp Paella (Pressure Cooked) 116
Mussels, Rice, and Potatoes (Slow Cooked) 118
Spicy Garlic-Ginger Shrimp (Slow Cooked) 120
Shrimp Alfredo (Pressure Cooked) 122
Quick Shrimp Risotto (Pressure Cooked) 124
Sweet-Spicy Salmon (Slow Cooked) 126
Thai-Style Cod w/ Pineapple Salsa (Pressure Cooked) ... 128

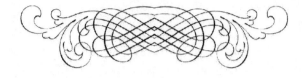

Easy Maple Salmon (Slow Cooked)

Serves: 6

Prep time: 1 minute
Cook time: 1 hour
Total time: 1 hour, 1 minute

I use a lot of savory herbs and spices on salmon, but once I used maple syrup, there was no going back. This is my favorite salmon recipe, which in addition to syrup, has lemon juice, soy sauce, garlic, and ginger. You can use either fresh salmon fillets, or frozen ones that have been thawed.

Ingredients:

5 (4-ounce) thawed (or fresh) salmon fillets
½ cup maple syrup
¼ cup soy sauce
⅛ cup lemon juice
3 minced garlic cloves
½ teaspoon ground ginger

Instructions:

1. Grease your Crock-Pot.
2. Lay down salmon in the pot.
3. Whisk together maple syrup, soy sauce, lemon juice, garlic, and ginger.
4. Pour over fish and close the lid.
5. Hit SLOW COOK and cook on high for 1 hour.

Nutritional Info (⅙ recipe):
Total calories: 426
Protein: 40
Carbs: 14.7
Fat: 22
Fiber: 0

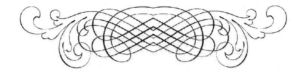

Creamy Haddock + Spinach (Pressure Cooked)

Serves: 4

Prep time: 6 minutes
Cook time: 6 minutes
Blend/sauce time: 6 minutes
Total time: 18 minutes

Haddock is a firm white fish with a mild flavor, so if you can't find, any white fish (like cod) will work. The star of this dish is the sauce, which is made from onion, garlic, tomatoes, stock, and cream, which you add *after* the pressure from the cooker has been released. The spinach is also added late in the recipe, because it wilts very quickly.

Cooking Note: If you don't like spinach, use another leafy green, like kale or collards.

Ingredients:

2 tablespoons butter
1 chopped onion
2 minced garlic cloves
2 cups chicken stock
2 cups whole + peeled canned tomatoes
1 tablespoon Italian seasoning
1 pound frozen (*not* thawed) haddock fillets
Salt to taste
2 cups fresh spinach
½ cup heavy cream

Instructions:

1. Hit BROWN/SAUTÉ on your Crock-Pot and add butter.
2. When melted and hot, add onion and garlic.
3. Cook until softened and fragrant.
4. Pour in chicken stock, and add tomatoes and Italian seasoning.
5. When simmering, lower in steamer basket and put haddock in it.
6. Season with salt and seal the lid.
7. Hit BEANS/CHILI and adjust time to 6 minutes.
8. When time is up, quick-release the pressure.
9. Remove the steamer basket.
10. Puree the broth with a hand blender (or in a regular blender).
11. Stir in spinach and cream, letting the heat from the broth wilt the leaves.
12. Serve fish with sauce!

Nutritional Info (¼ recipe):
Total calories: 216
Protein: 17
Carbs: 11
Fat: 9
Fiber: 1

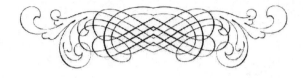

Shrimp Boil (Slow Cooked)

Serves: 6-8

Prep time: 1 minute
Cook time: 4 hours, 30-45 minutes
Total time: 4 hours, 31 minutes - 4 hours, 46 minutes

Shrimp boils are big on the East Coast, and can replace a traditional beef 'n pork BBQ. The potatoes cook first, because they take the longest, and it takes 4 hours on low with garlic, Old Bay seasoning, onions, and water. The corn, raw shrimp, sausage, and Old Bay seasoning are added, and the Crock-Pot runs for another 30-45 minutes, this time on high. Splitting up the ingredients when you're cooking means nothing gets overcooked.

Ingredients:

3 pounds red potatoes
4 minced garlic cloves
4 tablespoons Old Bay seasoning
2 sliced onions
4 cups water
2 ear's worth of corn kernels
1 ½ pounds raw shrimp
8-ounces sliced kielbasa sausage
¼ cup lemon juice
½ cup chopped parsley

Instructions:

1. Grease your Crock-Pot.
2. Put in potatoes, garlic, 2 tablespoons Old Bay seasoning, onions, and water.

3. Close the lid.
4. Hit SLOW COOK and cook on the low setting for 4 hours.
5. When time is up, open the lid.
6. Add corn, shrimp, sausage, and 2 tablespoons Old Bay seasoning.
7. Hit SLOW COOK again, this time cooking on high, for 30-45 minutes.
8. When shrimp is pink and solid, it's cooked through.
9. Mix in lemon juice and parsley.
10. Serve!

Nutritional Info (⅙ recipe):
Total calories: 468
Protein: 28
Carbs: 63
Fat: 12
Fiber: 7

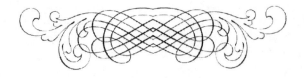

Shrimp Paella (Pressure Cooked)

<u>Serves:</u> 4

Prep time: 10 minutes
Cook time: 5 minutes
Shrimp time: 5 minutes
Total time: 20 minutes

Paella, a traditional Spanish dish, usually takes a long time to cook. When pressure cooked, it's just 20 minutes total. The aromatics cook first in plenty of butter, and then the rice is cooked in chicken stock and white wine. The shrimp, which should be purchased pre-cooked, heat up in the Crock-Pot.

Cooking Note: You'll notice that this recipe does not include saffron, which is the key ingredient in traditional paella. However, it's very expensive, and pretty much used for just this one dish, which is why I cut it out. Turmeric is an adequate substitute.

<u>Ingredients:</u>

- 4 tablespoons butter
- 1 chopped onion
- 4 minced garlic cloves
- 1 teaspoon paprika
- 1 teaspoon turmeric
- ¼ teaspoon red pepper flakes
- Salt to taste
- Black pepper to taste
- 1 cup dry Jasmine rice
- 1 cup chicken stock
- ½ cup white wine
- 1 pound cooked + thawed shrimp

Instructions:

1. Hit BROWN/SAUTÉ on your Crock-Pot and add butter.
2. When melted and hot, add onions.
3. When soft, add garlic and cook for another minute.
4. Stir in paprika, turmeric, red pepper flakes, salt, and black pepper.
5. After a minute, add rice and toast for half a minute or so, stirring constantly.
6. Pour in stock and wine. The rice should be covered.
7. Seal the lid.
8. Hit BEANS/CHILI and adjust time to 5 minutes.
9. When time is up, quick-release the pressure.
10. Stir in the thawed shrimp to warm through, using the leftover heat from the Crock-Pot.
11. When heated through, serve!

Nutritional Info (¼ recipe):
Total calories: 417
Protein: 28
Carbs: 44
Fat: 13
Fiber: 0

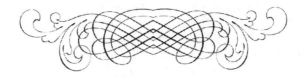

Mussels, Rice, and Potatoes (Slow Cooked)

<u>*Serves:*</u> 8

Prep time: 6 minutes
Steam time: 5 minutes
Cook time: 1 hour, 30 minutes
Total time: 1 hour, 41 minutes

You get a full meal in this recipe - mussels, potatoes, and rice. You cook the raw mussels first with onion and wine. After the liquid comes to a boil, you close the lid, but don't slow cook or pressure cook. Just let it boil for 5 minutes. The shells should open up, and the meat can be removed. Add mussel meat back into the cooker with potatoes, rice, dried parsley, and salt. It takes just 1 ½ hours on the high SLOW COOK setting.

Ingredients:

1 sliced onion
2 pounds raw mussels
1 cup white wine
2 pounds peeled + chopped potatoes
2 cups dry rice
Dried parsley to taste
Salt to taste

Instructions:

1. Grease your Crock-Pot.
2. Put onion slices to cover the bottom.
3. Add raw mussels and pour in white wine.
4. Hit BROWN/SAUTÉ and bring to a boil.
5. When boiling, cover the pot with a lid and wait 5 minutes.

6. The mussels should open.
7. Carefully remove the shells.
8. Add potatoes, rice, and mussels to the Crock-Pot.
9. Close the lid.
10. Hit SLOW COOK and cook on high for 1 ½ hours.
11. Add seasonings to taste, and serve!

Nutritional Info (⅛ recipe):
Total calories: 378
Protein: 19
Carbs: 64
Fat: 3
Fiber: 2.5

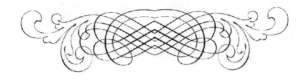

Spicy Garlic-Ginger Shrimp (Slow Cooked)

<u>Serves:</u> 4-6

Prep time: 1 minute
Cook time: 1 hour, 15 minutes
Additional time: 7 minutes
Total time: 1 hour, 23 minutes

This unique shrimp dish embraces the spicy side of life. The key ingredient is sambal oelek, which is an Indonesian hot sauce made from chili peppers, fish sauce, garlic, ginger, and more. Even though it has a fancy name, you can find it pretty much anywhere, even at Walmart. The sambal is cooked along with ginger, green onion, ketchup, garlic, apple cider vinegar, and sugar for 1 hour, so the sauce gets really blended. The shrimps are cooked shell-on next, for only 15 minutes. To finish the whole dish off, one beaten egg and sesame oil goes in, and cooks for another 7 minutes. The shrimp and sauce go wonderfully with rice!

Ingredients:

1 thumb minced ginger
1 minced green onion
5 minced garlic cloves
½ cup ketchup
2 tablespoons sambal oelek
2 tablespoons apple cider vinegar
1 tablespoon sugar
1 pound shell-on raw shrimp
1 tablespoon sesame oil
1 beaten egg

Instructions:

1. Grease your Crock-Pot.
2. Mix ginger, onion, garlic, ketchup, sambal oelek, vinegar, and sugar in the pot.
3. Close the lid.
4. Hit SLOW COOK and cook on the high setting for 1 hour.
5. When time is up, add shrimp.
6. Hit SLOW COOK again and cook on high for just 15 minutes.
7. When done, pour in sesame oil and egg.
8. Turn off the Crock-Pot, and replace the lid for another 7 minutes.
9. Serve!

Nutritional Info (¼ recipe):
Total calories: 291
Protein: 19
Carbs: 5
Fat: 5
Fiber: 0

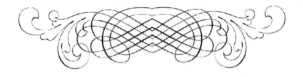

Shrimp Alfredo (Pressure Cooked)

<u>Serves:</u> 4-6

Prep time: 5 minutes
Cook time: 4 minutes
Sauce time: 5 minutes
Total time: 14 minutes

This recipe is one of my favorite ways to use shrimp when it's on sale. The only prep is cooking the garlic in some oil for a little while, so it's no longer raw. Next, add pasta and water into the pot. You actually cook the shrimp at the same time by wrapping it in a foil packet with salt, paprika, and lemon juice. It sits right on top of the pasta. Cook under pressure for just 4 minutes, and quick-release. Unwrap shrimp, mix into the pot, and pour in Alfredo sauce that's been mixed with sweet chili sauce.

<u>Ingredients:</u>

2 tablespoons olive oil
3 minced garlic cloves
1 pound pasta
3 cups water
1 pound raw shrimp
1 teaspoon salt
1 teaspoon paprika
1 tablespoon lemon juice
¾ of a 15-ounce jar of Alfredo sauce
½ cup sweet chili sauce

Instructions:

1. Hit BROWN/SAUTÉ on your crock-pot and add oil.
2. When hot, cook garlic until fragrant.
3. Put pasta in the pot (you'll have to break it in half) and add water.
4. Put raw shrimp on a piece of foil, and sprinkle with salt and paprika.
5. Drizzle on lemon juice.
6. Wrap foil around shrimp.
7. Stick right on top of pasta in the Crock-Pot and seal the lid.
8. Hit STEAM and adjust time to just 4 minutes on high pressure.
9. When time is up, do a quick-release right away.
10. Carefully remove shrimp packet, unwrap, and add shrimp to pasta.
11. To make sauce, mix Alfredo and sweet chili sauce together.
12. Stir into the pasta, letting the residual heat from the Crock-Pot warm up the whole thing.
13. Serve!

Nutritional Info (¼ recipe):
Total calories: 728
Protein: 39
Carbs: 101
Fat: 19
Fiber: 0

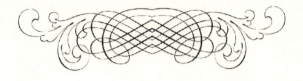

Quick Shrimp Risotto (Pressure Cooked)

<u>Serves</u>: 4

Prep time: 10 minutes
Cook time: 7 minutes
Shrimp time: 6 minutes
Total time: 23 minutes

Another favorite in my house, this shrimp risotto is bursting with buttery, cheesy flavors. The aromatics cook first to create that all-important base, and then you toast the rice. Deglaze with chicken and white wine, and then pressure cook for 7 minutes. The shrimp gets added after the pressure has been quick-released, and the heat from the rice heats the shrimp through.

<u>Ingredients:</u>

2 tablespoons butter
1 chopped onion
3 minced garlic cloves
1 cup dry Arborio rice
2 ¼ cups chicken stock
¼ cup white wine
2 teaspoons Italian seasoning
15 precooked + thawed shrimp
2 cups frozen peas
½ cup shredded Parmesan cheese
Salt to taste

Instructions:

1. Turn your Crock-Pot to BROWN/SAUTÉ and add butter.
2. When hot, add onions and garlic.
3. Cook until onions are clear.
4. Pour in rice and stir to toast for a minute or so.
5. Pour in chicken stock and wine, and sprinkle with Italian seasoning.
6. When simmering, seal the lid.
7. Hit BEANS/CHILI and adjust time to 7 minutes.
8. When time is up, quick-release and immediately add shrimp and peas.
9. Stir to cook the shrimp and warm the peas.
10. When shrimp is bright pink and solid looking, they're cooked.
11. Stir in cheese and taste, salting if needed.
12. Serve!

Nutritional Info (¼ recipe):
Total calories: 371
Protein: 18
Carbs: 50
Fat: 9
Fiber: 0

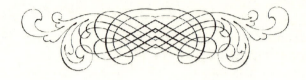

Sweet-Spicy Salmon (Slow Cooked)

<u>Serves:</u> 4

Prep time: 5 minutes
Cook time: 2 hours
Total time: 2 hours, 5 minutes

Honey is another sweet ingredient that goes really well with salmon, and it pairs with paprika, garlic, Italian seasoning, and chili powder in this recipe. Mix the spices with the honey, and slathered on four salmon fillets. Wrap in foil, and stick in the Crock-Pot to slow cook for 2 hours. Serve with rice!

Cooking Note: Cooking temperatures vary depending on the kind of salmon you're using. Wild salmon should be cooked to 120-degrees, while farmed salmon is best at 125.

<u>Ingredients:</u>

2 tablespoons honey
1 teaspoon paprika
2 minced garlic cloves
1 teaspoon Italian seasoning
½ teaspoon chili powder
½ teaspoon salt
Four (4-ounce) salmon fillets
4 cups cooked white rice

<u>Instructions:</u>

1. In a bowl, mix honey with the dry spices.
2. Lay out a piece of foil (one for each piece of fish), and lay down

fish.
3. Rub honey mixture evenly on all the fish and wrap up the fillets.
4. Put in your Crock-Pot.
5. Hit SLOW COOK and cook on the high setting for 2 hours, until salmon is 125-degrees.
6. Serve salmon with rice!

Nutritional Info (¼ recipe):
Total calories: 199
Protein: 24
Carbs: 21
Fat: 2
Fiber: 0

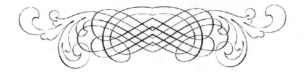

Thai-Style Cod w/ Pineapple Salsa (Pressure Cooked)

<u>Serves:</u> 4

Prep time: 30 minutes
Cook time: 10 minutes
Total time: 40 minutes

This is one of the few recipes that require marinating. I really can't recommend skipping this step, since it ensures the fish gets a lot of flavor. Once marinated in coconut milk, red curry paste, fish sauce, sweet chili sauce, garlic, and ginger, the fish gets wrapped in foil packets and put in a steamer basket. Pour 2 cups of water into the Crock-Pot, and lower in the basket. This pressure-cooks for 10 minutes on high. Serve the finished cod with pineapple salsa for a tropical treat!

<u>Ingredients:</u>

1 cup coconut milk
½ tablespoon Thai red curry paste
1 tablespoon fish sauce
2 teaspoons sweet chili sauce
3 minced garlic cloves
1 teaspoon ground ginger
4 cod fillets
2 cups water
Jar of pineapple salsa (like Newman's)

Instructions:

1. In a bowl, mix coconut milk, curry paste, fish sauce, chili sauce, garlic, and ginger.
2. Mix in a Ziploc bag with fish fillets and stick in the fridge for 30 minutes.
3. When ready, wrap fish fillets in individual foil packets.
4. Pour water into your cooker and insert a steamer basket.
5. Put fish packets in the basket and seal the lid.
6. Hit BEANS/CHILI and adjust time to 10 minutes on high pressure.
7. When time is up, quick-release the pressure.
8. Carefully unwrap fish and plate.
9. Serve with pineapple salsa!

Nutritional Info (¼ recipe):
Total calories: 182
Protein: 6
Carbs: 23
Fat: 11
Fiber: 1

Chapter 9: Soups + Stews

Because the Multi-Cooker is large, it's the perfect vehicle for making soups and stews. These get better with time, so I love making more than I need and saving the rest for leftovers. Slow cooked soups and stews are some of the best, because that long cooking time lets the flavors really blend and deepen. For pressure cooking the recipes, spices and browning certain ingredients become really important, because they don't have the benefit of time. Those stews are, however, really convenient when you want them hot and ready really quickly.

Chicken Potato Soup (Slow Cooked) *132*
Lasagna Soup (Slow Cooked) *134*
Beef Stew (Pressure Cooked) *136*
Parmesan Chicken Soup (Slow Cooked) *138*
Chicken Noodle Soup (Pressure Cooked) *140*
Creamy Chicken + Wild Rice Soup (Slow Cooked) *142*
Classic Tomato Soup (Pressure Cooked) *144*
Spiced Pumpkin Soup (Slow Cooked) *146*
Cheesy Cauliflower Soup (Pressure Cooked) *148*
Clam Chowder (Pressure Cooked) *150*

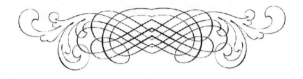

Chicken Potato Soup (Slow Cooked)

<u>*Serves:*</u> 6-8

Prep time: 5 minutes
Cook time: 8-12 hours
Total time: 8 hours, 5 minutes – 12 hours, 5 minutes

When I think about slow-cooked soups, this is the recipe that comes to mind. It has the four major aromatics: onion, garlic, carrots, and celery, so you know the flavors are going to be really savory and delicious. For the body of the soup, you've got chicken breasts and potatoes to fill you up. A little bacon never hurts, either.

Ingredients:

4 sliced cooked + chopped bacon
1 chopped onion
4 minced garlic cloves
1 ½ pounds boneless + skinless chicken breast
3 pounds peeled and sliced Yukon Gold potatoes
3 cups chopped carrots
2 cups chopped celery
8 cups chicken stock
1 teaspoon Italian seasoning
Salt to taste
Black pepper to taste
Splash of heavy cream

Instructions:

1. Grease your Crock-Pot.
2. Add bacon, onion, and garlic into the pot.

3. Put chicken breast on top, followed by potatoes, carrots, and celery.
4. Pour in the stock, and sprinkle in dry seasonings.
5. Close the lid.
6. Hit SLOW COOK and cook on the low setting for 8-12 hours.
7. Shred chicken and taste, seasoning with more salt and pepper if needed.
8. Add a splash of heavy cream to thicken.
9. Serve!

Nutritional Info (⅙ recipe):
Total calories: 393
Protein: 35
Carbs: 66
Fat: 5
Fiber: 6

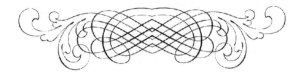

Lasagna Soup (Slow Cooked)

Serves: 8

Prep time: 12 minutes
Cook time: 7-8 hours
Additional time: 10 minutes
Total time: 7 hours, 22 minutes – 8 hours, 22 minutes

The classic pasta dish transforms into a soup overnight (or all day). It's got all the essential ingredients: beef, onion, garlic, tomatoes, pasta, and cheese. The beef is browned first with onion and garlic, and then cooks with tomatoes, tomato sauce, and beef stock. The pasta cooks separately, because it doesn't take long, and then you mix the whole thing together and top with cheese!

Ingredients:

1 pound ground beef
1 diced onion
4 minced garlic cloves
One (28-ounce) jar of crushed tomatoes
One (14.5-ounce) jar of Italian-style diced tomatoes
One (15-ounce) jar of tomato sauce
4 cups beef stock
4 teaspoons Italian seasoning
6-ounces dried pasta
Shredded parmesan cheese to taste
Shredded mozzarella cheese to taste

Instructions:

1. Hit BROWN/SAUTÉ on your cooker and add beef, onion, and garlic.
2. Stir to brown, until beef is no longer pink.
3. Add the rest of the ingredients up to the pasta - this cooks quickly, so it doesn't go in at this time.
4. Close the lid.
5. Hit SLOW COOK and cook on the low setting for 7-8 hours.
6. When there's 10 minutes or so left, cook the pasta in a pot on the stove.
7. When time is up on the Crock-Pot, add pasta and cook for another 10 minutes.
8. Serve soup with parmesan and mozzarella on top!

Nutritional Info (⅛ recipe):
Total calories: 240
Protein: 21
Carbs: 20
Fat: 9
Fiber: 1.8

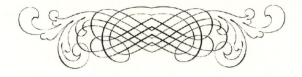

Beef Stew (Pressure Cooked)

Serves: 8

Prep time: 12 minutes
Cook time: 15-20 minutes
Natural pressure release: 10 minutes
Total time: 37-42 minutes

With beef stew, you usually have to plan a day ahead because it takes hours and hours. With the pressure cooking setting on the Multi-Cooker, you can make the stew in less than an hour. The major ingredients get browned first - onion, garlic, beef, carrots, and celery. That goes in the Crock-Pot with beef stock and potatoes, and cooks for just 15-20 minutes, until the beef is 145-degrees. To get a thicker consistency, add cornstarch slurry after pressure is released.

Ingredients:

1 tablespoon extra-virgin olive oil
1 diced onion
3 minced garlic cloves
2 pounds cubed beef stew meat
5 big diced carrots
3 diced celery stalks
2 cups beef stock
8 peeled and cubed potatoes
1 tablespoon cold water
2 teaspoons cornstarch
Salt to taste

Instructions:

1. Add oil to your Crock-Pot and hit BROWN/SAUTÉ.
2. When hot, add onion, garlic, and beef.
3. Stir and cook until beef is browned all over.
4. Add carrots and celery, and stir for a few minutes.
5. Pour in stock and add potatoes.
6. Seal the lid.
7. Hit BEANS/CHILI and adjust time to 15 minutes.
8. When time is up, wait for a natural pressure release.
9. Check meat - it should be 145-degrees.
10. If not, return to pressure for just 5 minutes. Quick-release.
11. Open the lid.
12. Mix cold water and cornstarch in a cup until smooth.
13. Pour into the Crock-Pot and stir to thicken.
14. Add salt to taste.
15. Serve hot!

Nutritional Info (⅛ recipe):

Total calories: 301
Protein: 30
Carbs: 32
Fat: 7
Fiber: 5.6

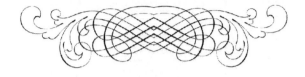

Parmesan Chicken Soup (Slow Cooked)

<u>Serves:</u> 4

Prep time: 10 minutes
Cook time: 7 hours, 25 minutes
Total time: 7 hours, 35 minutes

Parmesan is one of my favorite ingredients, and it's on display in this soup. After cooking garlic, onion, and celery in some olive oil, you slow cook chicken, tomatoes, chicken stock, Italian seasoning, and of course, parmesan cheese for 7 hours on the low temperature. The pasta is cooked for 25 minutes in the Crock-Pot. Soup's on!

<u>*Ingredients:*</u>

Glug of extra-virgin olive oil
4 minced garlic cloves
1 chopped onion
1 cup chopped celery
One (14.5-ounce) can of crushed tomatoes
2 boneless + skinless chicken breasts
5 cups chicken stock
1 cup shredded Parmesan
1 tablespoon Italian seasoning
4-ounces dry penne pasta
Salt to taste

<u>*Instructions:*</u>

1. Pour olive oil into your Crock-Pot and hit BROWN/SAUTÉ.
2. When hot, add garlic, onion, and celery.
3. Cook for a few minutes, until fragrant.

4. Add the rest of the ingredients through Italian seasoning.
5. Close the lid.
6. Hit SLOW COOK and cook on LOW for 7 hours.
7. When time is up, shred the chicken.
8. Stir in pasta.
9. Cook on SLOW COOK again, this time on HIGH, for 25 minutes.
10. Taste and salt if needed.
11. Serve!

Nutritional Info (¼ recipe):
Total calories: 299
Protein: 27
Carbs: 32
Fat: 8
Fiber: 1

CHAPTER 9: SOUPS + STEWS

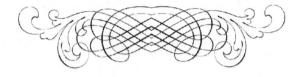

Chicken Noodle Soup (Pressure Cooked)

<u>*Serves:*</u> 4

Prep time: 10 minutes
Cook time: 7 minutes
Natural pressure release: 5 minutes
Noodle time: 5 minutes
Total time: 27 minutes

Someone in your family is feeling a bit under the weather, either physically or emotional. Whip up this super-quick chicken noodle soup that's brimming with carrots, celery, and old-fashioned savory flavors. It only takes about 30 minutes from start to finish!

<u>*Ingredients:*</u>

1 tablespoon extra-virgin olive oil
1 diced onion
4 minced garlic cloves
2 chopped carrots
2 chopped celery stalks
6 cups chicken stock
1 ½ pounds boneless + skinless chicken breast
8-ounces dry egg noodles
1 teaspoon dried parsley
Salt to taste
Black pepper to taste

<u>*Instructions:*</u>

1. Turn your Crock-Pot to BROWN/SAUTÉ and add oil.
2. When hot, add onion, garlic, carrots, and celery.

3. Cook until no longer raw and fragrant.
4. Pour in stock and deglaze by scraping up any stuck-0n food bits.
5. Add chicken and seal the lid.
6. Hit BEANS/CHILI and adjust time to 7 minutes.
7. When time is up, wait for a natural pressure release.
8. Shred the chicken.
9. Add noodles and hit BROWN/SAUTÉ again, to keep the soup warm.
10. Noodles should cook in about 5 minutes or so.
11. Taste and season the soup.
12. Serve!

Nutritional Info (¼ recipe):
Total calories: 460
Protein: 48
Carbs: 49
Fat: 7
Fiber: 1

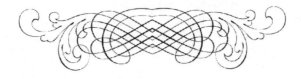

Creamy Chicken + Wild Rice Soup (Slow Cooked)

Serves: 10

Prep time: 1 minute
Cook time: 7-8 hours
Additional time: 5 minutes
Total time: 7 hours, 6 minutes – 8 hours, 6 minutes

Chicken and wild rice soup is my husband's favorite. His mom always used to make it, so it's a favorite of ours during "soup season," which is late autumn and through winter. There's really no prep to this recipe; just throw wild rice, boneless chicken breasts, onion, celery, carrots, stock and some dried herbs into the Crock-Pot. Cook on low for 7-8 hours. For the creaminess, heat a roux of butter, flour, and milk on the skillet, and mix into the Crock-Pot.

Ingredients:

1 cup dry wild rice
1 pound skinless + boneless chicken breasts
1 cup chopped onion
1 cup chopped celery
1 cup chopped carrots
6 cups chicken stock

½ teaspoon dried thyme
½ teaspoon dried parsley
½ cup butter
¾ cup flour
2+ cups whole milk
Salt to taste
Black pepper to taste

Instructions:

1. Pour rice, chicken, onion, celery, carrots, stock, thyme, and parsley into your Crock-Pot.

2. Stir and close the lid.
3. Hit SLOW COOK and cook on the low setting for 7-8 hours.
4. When time is up, shred the chicken.
5. In a skillet, melt butter and add flour.
6. When bubbling, wait a minute, and then whisk in the milk.
7. When all combined, pour into the Crock-Pot as a thickener and stir.
8. If too thick, add more milk.
9. Taste and season with salt and pepper as needed.
10. Serve!

Nutritional Info (1/10 recipe):
Total calories: 239
Protein: 15
Carbs: 17
Fat: 2
Fiber: 1

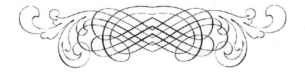

Classic Tomato Soup (Pressure Cooked)

Serves: 6

Prep time: 10 minutes
Cook time: 5 minutes
Natural pressure release: 5 minutes
Blend time: 5 minutes
Total time: 25 minutes

What's grilled cheese without tomato soup? This is a great recipe because it uses three kinds of tomatoes: canned ones, tomato paste, *and* sun-dried. That tomato flavor comes through really beautifully. Cook time is just 5 minutes, and then you blend it until perfectly-smooth.

Ingredients:

2 tablespoons butter
2 tablespoons extra-virgin olive oil
1 diced onion
2 minced garlic cloves
1 diced white potato
1 diced carrot
One (28-ounce) can of whole canned tomatoes
3 tablespoons tomato paste
3 tablespoons sun-dried tomatoes
4 cups vegetable stock
Salt to taste
Black pepper to taste

Instructions:

1. Turn your Crock-Pot to BROWN/SAUTÉ.
2. When hot, add butter and oil.
3. When that's hot, add onion and garlic.
4. Cook for a few minutes, then add potato and carrot.
5. Stir and cook for another few minutes.
6. Pour in canned tomato, tomato paste, sun-dried tomatoes, and stock.
7. Seal the lid.
8. Hit BEANS/CHILI and adjust time to just 5 minutes on high pressure.
9. When time is up, let the pressure come down naturally.
10. When pressure is gone, open the lid and blend soup with a hand blender or a regular blender until silky-smooth.
11. Taste and season with salt and pepper as needed.
12. Serve!

Nutritional Info (⅙ recipe):
Total calories: 156
Protein: 3
Carbs: 17
Fat: 9
Fiber: 1.6

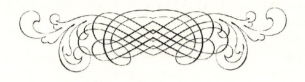

Spiced Pumpkin Soup (Slow Cooked)

<u>*Serves:*</u> 8

Prep time: 10 minutes
Cook time: 8-10 hours
Blend time: 5 minutes
Total time: 8 hours, 15 minutes – 10 hours, 15 minutes

I'm hit-or-miss on pumpkin, but I do love this recipe. I think it's the spices that really make it. In addition to the standard onion and garlic, you'll be adding cumin, paprika, nutmeg, and cloves. To get a really creamy texture, you're also adding a can of full-fat coconut milk. Everything cooks for 8-10 hours in the Crock-Pot, and then you puree. This is a great alternative to tomato soup and goes great with grilled cheese.

<u>*Ingredients:*</u>

1 tablespoon extra-virgin olive oil
1 diced onion
4 minced garlic cloves
1 tablespoon cumin
½ teaspoon paprika
½ teaspoon ground nutmeg
¼ teaspoon ground cloves
Salt to taste
Black pepper to taste
4 cups vegetable stock
One (29-ounce) can of pumpkin puree
One (14-ounce) can of full-fat unsweetened coconut milk

Instructions:

1. Turn your Crock-Pot to BROWN/SAUTÉ and add oil.
2. When hot, add onion and garlic.
3. Cook until onion is softened.
4. Add dry spices and stir for half a minute.
5. Pour in stock, puree, and coconut milk.
6. Close the lid.
7. Hit SLOW COOK and cook on the low setting for 8-10 hours.
8. When time is up, puree with a hand blender or in a regular blender.
9. Taste and add more seasonings as you like.
10. Serve!

Nutritional Info (⅛ recipe):

Total calories: 182
Protein: 1
Carbs: 15
Fat: 13
Fiber: 2.5

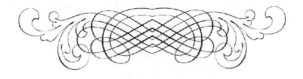

Cheesy Cauliflower Soup (Pressure Cooked)

<u>*Serves:*</u> 4

Prep time: 10 minutes
Cook time: 5 minutes
Natural pressure release: 5 minutes
Blend time: 5 minutes
Melt time: 5 minutes
Total time: 30 minutes

Not sure what to do with that head of cauliflower sitting in your fridge? Make it into a soup! Cook some aromatics (onion and garlic) in oil, and seal up the lid with cauliflower, stock, salt, and black pepper. After 5 minutes and a natural pressure release, puree with half-and-half, and then add cheese.

<u>*Ingredients:*</u>

2 teaspoons extra-virgin olive oil
1 diced onion
3 minced garlic cloves
1 head's worth of chopped cauliflower
1 ½ cups vegetable stock
Salt to taste
Black pepper to taste
1 cup half-and-half
⅔ cup grated mozzarella
½ cup grated parmesan

Instructions:

1. Hit BROWN/SAUTÉ on your Crock-Pot and add oil.
2. When hot, add onion and garlic, until fragrant and turning golden.
3. Add cauliflower, stock, salt, and pepper.
4. Seal the lid.
5. Hit BEANS/CHILI and adjust time to just 5 minutes on high pressure.
6. When time is up, wait for a natural pressure release.
7. Puree with an immersion blender or regular blender, adding in half-and-half.
8. Add cheese and stir until melted.
9. Serve!

Nutritional Info (¼ recipe):
Total calories: 233
Protein: 14
Carbs: 15
Fat: 14
Fiber: 5

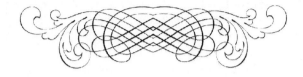

Clam Chowder (Pressure Cooked)

Serves: 4-6

Prep time: 20 minutes
Cook time: 5 minutes
Simmer time: 5 minutes
Total time: 30 minutes

Whenever I go to either coast, I have to get clam chowder, but that doesn't happen very often. To satisfy my craving, this pressure cooked recipe hits the spot. Pork belly, onion, salt, and pepper form an awesome flavor base that is essential to the rest of the soup, so do get the belly. Deglaze with white wine, and then add potatoes, seasonings, and clam juice. That cooks for just 5 minutes and gets a quick-release. The roux is your standard butter and flour, which goes in after pressure is released with half-and-half and clams. Serve with crusty bread!

Ingredients:

1 cup cubed pork belly
1 chopped onion
Salt to taste
Black pepper to taste
½ cup white wine
2 cubed white potatoes
1 teaspoon dried thyme
½ teaspoon Old Bay seasoning
2 cups clam juice
1 tablespoon butter
1 tablespoon flour
2 cups half-and-half
11-ounces canned clams

Instructions:

1. Put pork belly in your Crock-Pot and hit BROWN/SAUTÉ.
2. When sizzling, add onion, salt, and pepper.
3. Keep cooking until the onions have softened.
4. Pour in wine and deglaze, scraping up any stuck-on food bits.
5. When the wine is almost evaporated all the way, add potatoes, thyme, Old Bay seasoning, and clam juice.
6. Seal the lid.
7. Hit BEANS/CHILI and adjust time to just 5 minutes on high pressure.
8. To make your roux, melt butter in a skillet on the stove, and whisk in flour until blended.
9. When time is up on the Crock-Pot, quick-release the pressure.
10. Mix in the roux, half-and-half, and canned clams.
11. Hit BROWN/SAUTÉ on the Crock-Pot, and simmer for 5 minutes, with the lid off.
12. Serve!

Nutritional Info (¼ recipe):
Total calories: 345
Protein: 11
Carbs: 27
Fat: 21
Fiber: 4

Chapter 10: Vegan

There are two appliances that are must-haves for vegans: a slow cooker and a pressure cooker. With the Express Multi-Cooker, you get a Crock-Pot that's both! Both are really good at cooking ingredients like dry beans, lentils, and vegetables, and get the most flavor out of them. Pressure cooking is actually the healthiest cooking method and preserves the most nutrients, which is often a concern for vegans. This section contains recipes for both the slow cooker and pressure cooker setting on the Crock-Pot, and includes food from a variety of cuisines, so you never feel like you're eating the same thing all the time.

Quinoa-Bean Chili (Slow Cooked) *154*
Masala-Spiced Lentil Stew (Slow Cooked) *156*
Taco Bowl (Slow Cooked) *158*
Minestrone Soup (Pressure Cooked) *160*
Butternut Squash + Spinach Risotto (Pressure Cooked) *162*
Tofu + Rice (Slow Cooked) *164*
Coconut Tofu Curry (Pressure Cooked) *166*
Poached Pears (Pressure Cooked) *168*

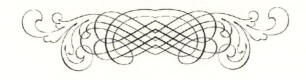

Quinoa-Bean Chili (Slow Cooked)

<u>Serves:</u> 6-8

Prep time: 1 minute
Cook time: 6-8 hours
Total time: 6 hours, 1 minute – 8 hours, 1 minute

Chili is one of the heartiest meals you can make in a Crock-Pot, and "veganizing" it isn't difficult. Instead of meat, you have two kinds of beans and quinoa. For flavoring, I like an organic taco seasoning that's free from preservatives and isn't too salty. Some dark cocoa powder add smokiness. Slow cook chili for 6-8 hours.

<u>Ingredients:</u>

5 cups veggie stock
2 (15-ounce) cans undrained black beans
2 (14-ounce) cans diced tomatoes
1 (15-ounce) can undrained pinto beans
1 cup raw quinoa
1 chopped onion
5 minced garlic cloves
3 tablespoons organic taco seasoning
Pinch of dark cocoa powder
Salt to taste

<u>Instructions:</u>

1. Pour everything into your Crock-Pot and give it a good stir.
2. Close the lid.
3. Hit SLOW COOK and cook on low for 6-8 hours.
4. Taste and season with more salt if needed.

5. Serve hot!

Nutritional Info (⅙ recipe):
Total calories: 315
Protein: 14
Carbs: 57
Fat: 3
Fiber: 11

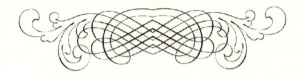

Masala-Spiced Lentil Stew (Slow Cooked)

<u>Serves:</u> 6-8

Prep time: 1 minute
Cook time: 6 hours
Total time: 6 hours, 1 minute

This stew is a great way to use dry lentils, which is a common meat substitute. The whole dish is spiced with garam masala, which is a staple Indian spice made from mace, cloves, peppercorns, cumin, coriander, and cinnamon. For creaminess, you add a cup of coconut milk before serving.

Cooking Note: Bee Free Honee is a brand that makes a honey substitute from apples, cane sugar, and lemon juice.

<u>Ingredients:</u>

4 cups veggie stock
2 ½ cups dry brown lentils
1 (15-ounce) can undrained diced tomatoes
¼ cup tomato paste
1 ½ teaspoons garam masala
1 teaspoon Bee-Free honey
1 teaspoon garlic powder
1 teaspoon onion powder
1 teaspoon ground ginger
Salt to taste
1 cup lite coconut milk

Instructions:

1. Put all the ingredients (minus coconut milk) in your Crock-Pot and stir.
2. Hit SLOW COOK and cook on low for 6 hours. Check after 4 hours to see if the lentils have soaked up too much liquid. If so, add some more stock and finish cooking.
3. When time is up, stir in coconut milk.
4. Serve as is or over rice!

Nutritional Info (⅙ recipe):

Total calories: 355
Protein: 23
Carbs: 58
Fat: 4
Fiber: 12.5

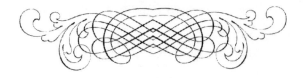

Taco Bowl (Slow Cooked)

<u>**Serves:**</u> 6

Prep time: 1 minute
Cook time: 2 hours
Total time: 2 hours, 1 minute

A relatively short recipe for the slow cooker setting on the Crock-Pot, this taco bowl contains all the must-haves, like beans, salsa, bell pepper, and rice. To top things off, a sliced avocado brings in healthy fats. I like this recipe because it's versatile, and you can use different ingredients to change things up, like using different kinds of beans, vegetables, and salsas.

<u>*Ingredients:*</u>

2 cups vegetable stock
1 cup long-grain brown rice
1 chopped onion
Salt to taste
½ tablespoon organic taco seasoning
2 (15-ounce) cans drained black beans
1 chopped yellow bell pepper
5 cups salsa (your choice of heat)
1 sliced avocado

<u>*Instructions:*</u>

1. Mix stock, rice, onion, salt, and taco seasoning in your greased Crock-Pot.
2. Cook on SLOW COOK for 1 ½ hours on the high setting.
3. When that time is up, add drained black beans and bell pepper, and mix.

4. Cook for another 30 minutes.
5. When ready, serve with salsa and avocado!

Nutritional Info (⅙ recipe):
Total calories: 346
Protein: 12
Carbs: 64
Fat: 2
Fiber: 14

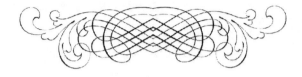

Minestrone Soup (Pressure Cooked)

<u>*Serves:*</u> 8-10

Prep time: 6 minutes
Cook time: 30 minutes
Pasta time: 6 minutes
Total time: 42 minutes

A classic Italian soup, minestrone is essentially vegan already. It's a great way to use up vegetables. In this recipe, you use green beans, tomatoes, potatoes, zucchini, and chickpeas. Like with most recipes that use the pressure cooking setting, you want to create a flavor base by cooking garlic and onion in olive oil before adding other ingredients. This deepens the flavor, and makes it taste like it's been cooking much longer. Pasta goes in the soup *after* it's been brought to pressure and the pressure's been released, because pasta cooks very quickly.

<u>*Ingredients:*</u>

4 tablespoons extra-virgin olive oil
5 minced garlic cloves
1 diced sweet onion
6 cups veggie stock
1 cup chopped green beans
2 (14.5-ounce) cans diced tomatoes
2 chopped potatoes
1 diced zucchini
1 (15.5-ounce) can of drained chickpeas
3 teaspoons Italian seasoning
Salt to taste
Black pepper to taste
1 cup dry elbow macaroni

Instructions:

1. Turn your Crock-Pot to BROWN/SAUTÉ and pour in olive oil.
2. Cook garlic and onion until fragrant.
3. Turn off the cooker.
4. Pour in your stock, making sure it's at or below the "max" line, then add in the rest of the ingredients (*except* macaroni).
5. Give it a good stir.
6. Seal the lid.
7. Hit BEANS/CHILI and adjust time to 30 minutes.
8. When time is up, turn off the cooker and quick-release the pressure.
9. Pour dry pasta into the soup and wait. The heat will cook the pasta, and when it's at the texture you want, it's time to serve!
10. Taste and add more seasonings if needed.

Nutritional Info (⅛ recipe):
Total calories: 238
Protein: 7
Carbs: 34
Fat: 8
Fiber: 13

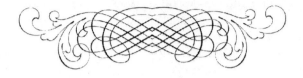

Butternut Squash + Spinach Risotto (Pressure Cooked)

<u>Serves:</u> 4-6

Prep time: 10 minutes
Cook time: 5 minutes
Total time: 15 minutes

A rich risotto flavored with garlic, thyme, and nutmeg, this recipe can be eaten as a meal or as a side. Most of the time it takes to make the risotto is actually just prepping the ingredients by cooking them in olive oil to bring out their flavors. The actual cook time under pressure is just 5 minutes. Spinach is the last ingredient you add, because the heat is enough to wilt the leaves.

Ingredients:

2 tablespoons extra-virgin olive oil
4 minced garlic cloves
4 cups diced butternut squash
2 cups dry Arborio rice
¼ cup white wine
4 cups veggie stock
2 teaspoons dried thyme
2 teaspoons salt
2 cups fresh spinach
1 teaspoon ground nutmeg

Instructions:

1. Add olive oil to your Crock-Pot and hit BROWN/SAUTÉ.
2. Cook garlic until fragrant and turning golden.
3. Remove and plate for now.
4. Add squash and turn to coat.
5. Leave be for 4 minutes to roast on one side.
6. Add rice and toast for 2 minutes or so.
7. Pour in wine and wait until it has evaporated before pouring in veggie stock, dried thyme, salt, and the cooked garlic.
8. Seal the lid.
9. Hit BEANS/CHILI and adjust time to 5 minutes on high pressure.
10. When time is up, turn off the cooker and quick-release.
11. Add spinach and mix the risotto well, letting the heat wilt the leaves.
12. Serve with a sprinkle of nutmeg.

Nutritional Info (¼ recipe):
Total calories: 431
Protein: 8
Carbs: 87
Fat: 7
Fiber: 3

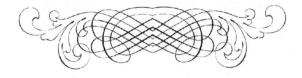

Tofu + Rice (Slow Cooked)

Serves: 4

Prep time: 5 minutes
Cook time: 7-9 hours
Thicken time: 5 minutes
Total time: 7 hours, 10 minutes – 9 hours, 10 minutes

The vegan version of chicken and rice, this recipe substitutes the meat with tofu. It's cooked in a sauce made of coconut aminos, rice vinegar, Bee-Free honey, nutritional yeast, ginger, and garlic salt. For a side, there are chopped carrots, too. The meal is slow-cooked for 7-9 hours, after which the sauce is thickened with cornstarch and served with cooked brown rice!

Ingredients:

½ cup water
¼ cup coconut aminos
½ tablespoon rice vinegar
3 tablespoons Bee-Free honey
3 tablespoons nutritional yeast
1 teaspoon ground ginger
1 teaspoon garlic salt
1 cup chopped carrots
14-ounces cubed extra-firm tofu
2 tablespoons cold water
1 teaspoon cornstarch
4 cups cooked brown rice

Instructions:

1. Mix water, coconut aminos, rice vinegar, Bee-Free honey, yeast, ginger, and garlic salt together in a bowl.
2. Grease your Crock-Pot.
3. Put your carrots in the Crock-Pot, and then add tofu.
4. Pour over the sauce and close the lid.
5. Cook on SLOW COOK for 7-9 hours.
6. When time is up, mix water and cornstarch together.
7. Turn the Crock-Pot to BROWN/SAUTÉ and whisk in the water/cornstarch mixture.
8. Sauce will thicken.
9. Serve with brown rice!

Nutritional Info (¼ recipe):
Total calories: 388
Protein: 18
Carbs: 67
Fat: 7
Fiber: 4.5

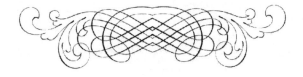

Coconut Tofu Curry (Pressure Cooked)

<u>Serves:</u> 4

Prep time: 6 minutes
Cook time: 5 minutes
Total time: 11 minutes

One of the best ways to prepare tofu is with a sauce made from full-fat coconut milk, peanut butter, and curry powder. Tofu is bland on its own, so a flavorful sauce is really important. The sauce also includes onion, tomato sauce, and spices. Cook time is just 4 minutes on the STEAM setting, followed by a quick-release. It takes less than 15 minutes to make!

Ingredients:

10-ounces full-fat coconut milk
2 tablespoons creamy peanut butter
1 tablespoon mild curry powder
1 cup chopped onion
8-ounces tomato sauce
2 sliced scallions
1 teaspoon salt
1 teaspoon onion powder
½ teaspoon ground ginger
Pinch of cayenne pepper (optional: if you want more heat)
½ cup veggie stock
1 cup extra-firm diced tofu

Instructions:

1. To make the curry sauce, blend everything except tofu and stock until smooth.

2. Taste and adjust seasonings to your liking.
3. Grease your Crock-Pot and put in the tofu.
4. Pour in stock and sauce.
5. Seal the lid.
6. Cook on STEAM for 4 minutes.
7. When time is up, turn off the Crock-Pot and quick-release the pressure.
8. Serve!

Nutritional Info (¼ recipe):
Total calories: 237
Protein: 5
Carbs: 11
Fat: 21
Fiber: 1

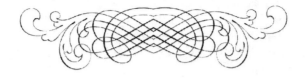

Poached Pears (Pressure Cooked)

Serves: 6

Prep time: 6 minutes
Cook time: 4 minutes
Total time: 10 minutes

Vegan desserts can be tricky, and often use expensive substitutes. This recipe is simple and perfect for winter, when pears are in season. Simmer grape juice and sugar together to make a syrup, and then add pears rubbed with lemon. Cook for just 4 minutes, and then quick-release the pressure. The pears will be soft, the syrup thick and sweet. Finish off the dessert with a sprinkle of cinnamon, nutmeg, and ginger.

Ingredients:

5 cups white grape juice
½ cup white sugar
6 firm + ripe peeled pears
1 halved lemon
1 teaspoon ground cinnamon
½ teaspoon ground nutmeg
¼ teaspoon ground ginger

Instructions:

1. Pour grape juice and sugar into your Crock-Pot.
2. Turn on the BROWN/SAUTÉ setting.
3. Bring to a simmer, letting the sugar dissolve completely.
4. Hit the KEEP WARM button.
5. Slice the bottom off the pears, so they stand on their own.
6. Rub the pear flesh with lemon juice.

7. Put pears and lemon in the Crock-Pot, and seal the lid.
8. Hit STEAM and adjust time to 4 minutes.
9. When time is up, quick-release the pressure.
10. Plate the pears, drizzling on syrup.
11. Sprinkle pears with spices and serve!

Nutritional Info (⅙ recipe):
Total calories: 319
Protein: 1
Carbs: 80
Fat: 0
Fiber: 6

Chapter 11: Sides + Snacks

You have a gathering coming up, and everyone needs to bring a snack or a side. You could swing by the store and grab one of those meat-and-cheese platters, but why not make something way tastier and just as easy? In the Crock-Pot, you can make a wide range of dips and sides that everyone will be asking about. If something spontaneous comes up and you don't have time to cook overnight, the pressure cooker function comes to the rescue. This section is full of party staples like buffalo chicken and queso dip, as well as more unique side dishes like pinto beans with pork belly and mushrooms marinated in red wine.

Buffalo Chicken Dip (Slow Cooked) *172*
Buffalo Chicken Wings (Pressure Cooked) *174*
Simple Spinach Dip (Slow Cooked) *176*
Hummus (Pressure Cooked) *178*
Red-Wine Mushrooms (Slow Cooked) *180*
Pork Pinto Beans (Pressure Cooked) *182*
Queso Dip (Slow Cooked) *184*
Crab Party Dip (Slow Cooked) *186*
Sweet 'n Sour Turkey Meatballs (Pressure Cooked) *188*
Easy Veggie Rice (Pressure Cooked) *190*

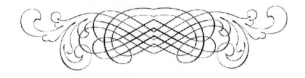

Buffalo Chicken Dip (Slow Cooked)

<u>Serves:</u> 8-10

Prep time: 5 minutes
Cook time: 2 hours
Total time: 2 hours, 5 minutes

With a total time of just over 2 hours, this recipe for buffalo chicken dip is perfect for watching a big game with friends. Creamy, cheesy, and with that unforgettable bleu cheese bite, you're sure to have friends asking how you made it. Serve with tortilla chips.

Ingredients:

16-ounces cream cheese
2 cups cooked + shredded chicken
1 cup hot sauce
1 cup bleu cheese dressing
1 ½ cups shredded mozzarella

Instructions:

1. Grease your Crock-Pot.
2. Put cream cheese and 1 cup of chicken in the pot.
3. Pour in ½ cup hot sauce and ½ cup bleu cheese dressing.
4. Add the rest of the chicken, hot sauce, and dressing, in layers.
5. Top with shredded mozzarella.
6. Close the lid.
7. Hit SLOW COOK and cook on LOW for 2 hours.
8. Serve!

Nutritional Info (⅛ recipe):
Total calories: 476
Protein: 22
Carbs: 7
Fat: 42
Fiber: 0

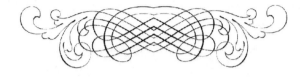

Buffalo Chicken Wings (Pressure Cooked)

Serves: 6

Prep time: 1 minute
Cook time: 10 minutes
Natural pressure release: 10 minutes
Broil time: 5 minutes
Total time: 26 minutes

Need a quick appetizer or snack food to share? At just under 30 minutes, these chicken wings have almost no prep time, and are big on flavor. You make your own buffalo sauce using hot sauce and butter, which you pour over wings that have been pressure cooked for just 10 minutes. To get a crispier skin, broil for 5 minutes.

Ingredients:

1 cup water
2 pounds boneless chicken wings
¼ cup hot sauce
¼ cup melted butter
¼ teaspoon paprika
⅛ teaspoon cayenne pepper
Salt to taste
Black pepper to taste

Instructions:

1. Pour water into your Crock-Pot and lower in steamer basket.
2. Put wings in the basket.
3. Seal the lid.
4. Hit BEANS/CHILI and adjust time to 10 minutes on high

pressure.
5. When time is up, wait for a natural pressure release.
6. While the pressure goes down, mix hot sauce, butter, and seasonings.
7. Move chicken to a bowl, and pour over sauce.
8. With kitchen clamps, turn so the sauce coats chicken evenly.
9. For a crispy exterior, move to a sheet pan and broil for just 5 minutes.
10. Serve with ranch or bleu cheese dressing!

Nutritional Info (⅙ recipe):
Total calories: 297
Protein: 34
Carbs: 0
Fat: 17
Fiber: 0

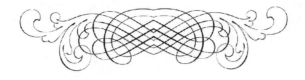

Simple Spinach Dip (Slow Cooked)

Serves: 4-6

Prep time: 1 minute
Cook time: 2 hours
Total time: 2 hours, 1 minute

Even people who don't like spinach like spinach dip. That's probably because of ingredients like cream cheese and shredded cheese. All the ingredients go in your Crock-Pot and cook for 2 hours. Season to your liking with paprika, red pepper flakes, salt, and pepper.

Ingredients:

10-ounces frozen + thawed spinach
8-ounces cream cheese
1 cup shredded mozzarella
½ cup shredded parmesan
3 minced garlic cloves
½ teaspoon paprika
½ teaspoon red pepper flakes
Salt to taste
Black pepper to taste

Instructions:

1. Grease your Crock-Pot.
2. Add all the ingredients.
3. Close the lid.
4. Hit SLOW COOK and cook on the HIGH setting for just 2 hours.
5. Stir and taste, adding more seasoning if needed.
6. Serve with crusty bread!

Nutritional Info (¼ recipe):
Total calories: 329
Protein: 16
Carbs: 4
Fat: 29
Fiber: 1

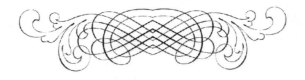

Hummus (Pressure Cooked)

Serves: 10-12

Prep time: *1 minute*
Cook time: *35 minutes*
Natural pressure release: *15 minutes*
Blend time: *5 minutes*
Chill time: *2 hours*
Total time: *2 hours, 56 minutes*

Hummus is an ancient food, but it's taken a while for the West to really get into it. Now, you can find it everywhere, but it's not always the cheapest item. You can make your own for much less and in bigger batches. Pressure cook chickpeas and water with olive oil for just 35 minutes, and wait for a natural pressure release. Next, you puree with tahini (sesame paste), lemon juice, and garlic until you get a creamy, smooth texture. You can serve the dip warm or cold.

Ingredients:

8 cups water
2 cups dried chickpeas
6 tablespoons extra-virgin olive oil
½ cup tahini
6 tablespoons lemon juice
5 minced garlic cloves
Salt to taste
Dash of paprika

Instructions:

1. Pour water into your Crock-Pot, and add chickpeas and 2 tablespoons of olive oil.
2. Seal the lid.
3. Hit BEANS/CHILI and adjust time to 35 minutes on high pressure.
4. When time is up, wait for a natural pressure release.
5. When it's okay to open the lid, strain the chickpeas and save ½ cup liquid.
6. Move chickpeas to a food processor and puree.
7. Add ½ cup cooking liquid, along with the tahini, lemon juice, garlic, and salt.
8. Keep pureeing until smooth.
9. Stir in the rest of the olive oil, add a dash of paprika, and move to a container.
10. Store in fridge under cling wrap for 2 hours.
11. Serve!

Nutritional Info (1/10 recipe):
Total calories: 233
Protein: 8
Carbs: 26
Fat: 16
Fiber: 7

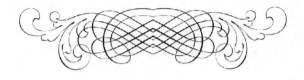

Red-Wine Mushrooms (Slow Cooked)

Serves: 10-12

Prep time: 5 minutes
Cook time: 12 hours
Total time: 12 hours, 5 minutes

Perfect as a snack, side, or hamburger topping, these mushrooms cook for a lengthy 12 hours and get fully-infused with flavors from wine, dill, garlic, and Worcestershire. I could eat these mushrooms all day long. One batch makes enough for 10-12 people.

Ingredients:

4 pounds button mushrooms
2 cups chicken stock
1 cup red wine
1 teaspoon ground dill
1 teaspoon garlic powder
1 teaspoon Worcestershire sauce
½ cup butter
Salt to taste

Instructions:

1. Grease your Crock-Pot.
2. Add mushrooms.
3. In a bowl, mix stock, wine, and seasonings.
4. Add butter on top.
5. Close the lid.
6. Hit SLOW COOK and cook on the lowest temperature setting for 12 hours.

7. Enjoy!

Nutritional Info (1/10 recipe):
Total calories: 140
Protein: 6
Carbs: 6
Fat: 10
Fiber: 2

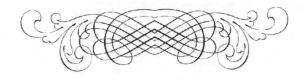

Pork Pinto Beans (Pressure Cooked)

<u>Serves:</u> 6

Prep time: 15 minutes
Cook time: 35 minutes
Natural pressure release: 25 minutes
Simmer time: 5 minutes
Total time: 1 hour, 20 minutes

You need to bring a side for a BBQ, and you don't want to just buy something at the store. This recipe is perfect, and turns dried beans into a delicious, flavorful dish in less than 2 hours. The pork belly is the secret ingredient, and adds amazing layers of rich, fatty flavors that the pinto beans soak up during cooking.

<u>Ingredients:</u>

1 tablespoon extra-virgin olive oil
4-ounces cubed pork belly
1 diced onion
3 minced garlic cloves
2 cups dry pinto beans
3 cups chicken stock
15-ounces canned tomatoes
Salt to taste
Black pepper to taste

<u>Instructions:</u>

1. Add oil to your Crock-Pot and heat on BROWN/SAUTÉ.
2. When hot, add pork belly.
3. Cook until sizzling and beginning to brown on the edges.

4. Add onion and garlic.
5. Keep cooking until onion is softening.
6. Pour in beans and stir for half a minute.
7. Pour in stock, stir, and seal the lid.
8. Hit BEANS/CHILI and adjust time to 35 minutes on high pressure.
9. When time is up, wait for a natural pressure release.
10. Pour in tomatoes.
11. Hit BROWN/SAUTÉ again and let the pot simmer.
12. When liquid is thickened, the beans are ready!
13. Add salt and pepper to taste.

Nutritional Info (⅙ recipe):
Total calories: 233
Protein: 9
Carbs: 21
Fat: 12
Fiber: 5

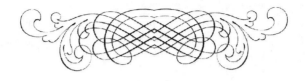

Queso Dip (Slow Cooked)

Serves: 6-8

Prep time: 10 minutes
Cook time: 1 hour, 30 minutes
Total time: 1 hour, 40 minutes

When I'm making tacos for dinner, I always make this queso dip as a starter/side. It tastes so much better than store-bought, and for a slow cooker recipe, it's very short. You cook onion, garlic, and green chiles first, just so they aren't raw anymore, and then slow cook cheeses, milk, and cream cheese for 1 ½ hours on the low temperature setting. This stuff is like liquid gold.

Ingredients:

1 tablespoon extra-virgin olive oil
1 diced onion
3 minced garlic cloves
4-ounces drained and minced green chiles
2 ½ cups shredded Mexican cheese
½ cup shredded mozzarella
8-ounces cream cheese
½ cup whole milk
Salt to taste

Instructions:

1. Hit BROWN/SAUTÉ on your Crock-Pot and add oil.
2. When hot, add onion, garlic, and chiles.
3. Cook until onion is beginning to soften.
4. Add cheese, cream cheese, and milk.

5. Stir before closing the lid.
6. Hit SLOW COOK and adjust time to 1 ½ hours on LOW.
7. When time is up, open the lid and stir.
8. If it's too thick, add milk as needed.
9. Add salt to taste.
10. Serve!

Nutritional Info (⅙ recipe):
Total calories: 379
Protein: 16
Carbs: 7
Fat: 32
Fiber: 0

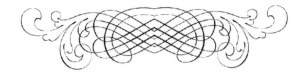

Crab Party Dip (Slow Cooked)

<u>*Serves:*</u> 6

Prep time: 1 minute
Cook time: 2 hours
Total time: 2 hours, 1 minute

Crab dip is a snack I see a lot at sports bars, but I didn't think about making it myself until I learned it's easily done in a Crock-Pot with canned crab meat. It's a great option when you're tired of the usual chicken or bean-based dips, and are craving seafood. Everything goes in the Crock-Pot at once - cheese, mayo, garlic, lemon juice, soy sauce, Old Bay, crab - and cooks for just 2 hours on the low setting. Stir, and it's ready!

<u>Ingredients:</u>

12-ounces cream cheese
½ cup shredded parmesan
½ cup mayonnaise
3 minced garlic cloves
One lemon's worth of juice
1 tablespoon soy sauce
1 teaspoon Old Bay seasoning
12-ounces drained crab meat

<u>Instructions:</u>

1. Grease your Crock-Pot.
2. Add cream cheese, parmesan, mayo, garlic, lemon juice, soy sauce, Old Bay seasoning, and crab meat.
3. Stir.
4. Close the lid.

5. Hit SLOW COOK and cook on the low setting for 2 hours.
6. When time is up, stir again and serve!

Nutritional Info (⅙ recipe):
Total calories: 398
Protein: 16
Carbs: 3
Fat: 36
Fiber: 0

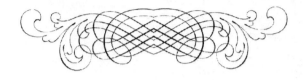

Sweet 'n Sour Turkey Meatballs (Pressure Cooked)

Serves: 4

Prep time: 10 minutes
Cook time: 6 minutes
Natural pressure release: 6 minutes
Sauce time: 5 minutes
Total time: 27 minutes

Sweet 'n sour sauce is one of my favorite things in the world, and turkey is a really good meat to pair it with, because it isn't too heavy, and the sauce keeps the meat moist. The meatballs are made with ground turkey, egg, onion, and bread crumbs. Simple! The sauce is ketchup, brown sugar, rice vinegar, pineapples and pineapple juice, and soy sauce. After browning the meatballs, they cook in the sauce for just 6 minutes. To thicken the sauce, you use cornstarch after a natural pressure release.

Ingredients:

1 pound ground turkey
1 egg
1 cup diced onion
1 cup panko bread crumbs
½ cup ketchup
½ cup brown sugar
½ cup rice vinegar
2 cups canned pineapple w/ juice
2 tablespoons soy sauce
Salt to taste
Black pepper to taste

1 tablespoon extra-virgin olive oil
¼ cup water
2 tablespoons cornstarch

Instructions:

1. Mix turkey, egg, onion, and breadcrumbs.
2. Form into 1-inch meatballs.
3. In a bowl, mix ketchup, sugar, rice vinegar, pineapple, juice, soy sauce, salt, and pepper.
4. Pour oil into your Crock-Pot and hit BROWN/SAUTÉ.
5. Add meatballs, and brown all over.
6. Pour in sauce and seal the lid.
7. Hit BEANS/CHILI and adjust time to 6 minutes on high pressure.
8. When time is up, wait for a natural pressure release.
9. In a bowl, mix water and cornstarch until smooth.
10. Hit BROWN/SAUTÉ on your Crock-Pot again and pour in slurry.
11. Stir until sauce has thickened.
12. Serve!

Nutritional Info (¼ Recipe):
Total calories: 335
Protein: 18
Carbs: 49
Fat: 9
Fiber: 0

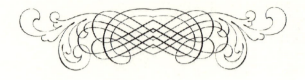

Easy Veggie Rice (Pressure Cooked)

Serves: 4-6

Prep time: 10 minutes
Cook time: 3 minutes
Natural pressure release: 6 minutes
Total time: 19 minutes

Everyone needs a tasty, easy rice side dish they can pair with any meal. This one takes less than a half hour, and is full of fresh veggies like carrots, zucchini, and bell peppers. You can use any vegetables that are in season. Cook time is just 3 minutes! Wait for a natural pressure release before serving.

Ingredients:

1 tablespoon extra-virgin olive oil
1 chopped onion
1 chopped yellow bell pepper
1 chopped carrot
1 chopped zucchini
Water as needed
2 cups long-grain rice
½ cup frozen peas
Salt to taste
Black pepper to taste

Instructions:

1. Hit BROWN/SAUTÉ on your Crock-Pot and add oil.
2. When hot, add onion and cook until clear.
3. Take a 1-liter measuring cup and add bell pepper, carrot, and

zucchini.
4. Add enough water to hit the 3-cup mark.
5. Pour rice, peas, salt, and pepper into your Crock-Pot.
6. Pour measuring cup with water and veggies into the pot and stir.
7. Seal the lid.
8. Hit STEAM and adjust time to 5 minutes on low pressure.
9. When time is up, wait for a natural pressure release.
10. Taste rice and add more salt if needed before serving!

Nutritional Info (¼ recipe):
Total calories: 429
Protein: 9
Carbs: 85
Fat: 4
Fiber: 1

Chapter 12: Condiments

Your Crock-Pot can be used for more than just full meals, desserts, or side dishes. You can make essential pantry staples like spaghetti sauce and hot sauce, and special condiments like bacon jam. When you make these types of ingredients at home, you save money in the long-run, *and* you have total control of what goes into them. Refined sugar is the most common additive to store-bought condiments, and it fuels an addiction that we all wish we could curb. Using your Crock-Pot's slow cooker and pressure cooker settings, you can make healthier (and tastier) versions, and never have to buy ketchup again!

Spaghetti Sauce (Slow Cooked)...*194*
Bolognese Sauce (Pressure Cooked).....................................*196*
Homemade Ketchup (Slow Cooked)...................................... *198*
Habanero Hot Sauce (Pressure Cooked) *200*
Serrano Relish (Slow Cooked) *202*
Caramelized Onions (Pressure Cooked).........................*204*
Bacon Jam (Slow Cooked) *206*
Maple-Chipotle BBQ Sauce (Pressure Cooked)..............*208*

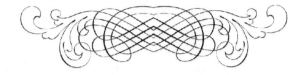

Spaghetti Sauce (Slow Cooked)

Serves: 10

Prep time: 1 minute
Cook time: 3-4 hours
Total time: 3 hours, 1 minute – 4 hours, 1 minute

Spaghetti sauce is one of those ingredients you *always* need, but there are so many brands to choose from. For a rich homemade sauce with no added sugar, look no further than this recipe. It makes enough sauce for 10 people, and it's easily doubled if you want to make a lot at once to store in your fridge. All you need is tomatoes, an onion, garlic, Italian seasoning, salt, and tomato paste

Cooking Note: You can use fresh tomatoes, but most agree that you actually get better flavor from high-quality canned tomatoes.

Ingredients:

8 cups diced tomatoes
1 big chopped onion
4 minced garlic cloves
1 tablespoon Italian seasoning
Salt to taste
1 (6-ounce) can tomato paste

Instructions:

1. Grease your Crock-Pot.
2. Put in the ingredients through salt and close the lid.
3. Cook on SLOW COOK for 3-4 hours on the low setting, stirring every hour.

4. When time is up, taste and add more seasonings if needed.
5. Mash up tomatoes if you like a smoother sauce.
6. Stir in tomato paste to thicken sauce before serving.

Nutritional Info (1/10 serving):
Total calories: 70
Protein: 3
Carbs: 14
Fat: 0
Fiber: 1.7

CHAPTER 12: CONDIMENTS

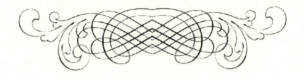

Bolognese Sauce (Pressure Cooked)

Serves: 10

Prep time: 10 minutes
Cook time: 15 minutes
Natural pressure release: 10 minutes
Total time: 35 minutes

Traditional Bolognese sauce takes plain old ground beef and transforms it into Italy on a plate. This recipe has you cook some essential aromatics first - onions and carrots - before browning the beef and deglazing with white wine. 2 cans of diced tomatoes go into the Crock-Pot, and the whole thing cooks under pressure for just 15 minutes. Stir in half-and-half for added richness, and your sauce is ready to serve!

Ingredients:

1 tablespoon extra-virgin olive oil
1 minced onion
2 chopped carrots
2 pounds ground beef
¼ cup dry white wine
2 (28-ounce) cans diced tomatoes
½ cup half-and-half
Italian seasoning to taste
Salt to taste

Instructions:

1. Hit BROWN/SAUTÉ on your Crock-Pot and add oil.
2. When hot, add onion and carrots.
3. Stir and cook until softened.

4. Add beef and brown.
5. When pink is gone, pour in wine and cook for 4 minutes.
6. Add tomatoes and seal the lid.
7. Hit BEANS/CHILI and adjust time to 15 minutes on high pressure.
8. When time is up, wait for a natural pressure release.
9. When the pressure is gone, open the lid and add half-and-half.
10. Taste and season to taste.
11. The sauce is ready!

Nutritional Info (1/10 serving):
Total calories: 207
Protein: 21
Carbs: 9
Fat: 10
Fiber: 2

CHAPTER 12: CONDIMENTS

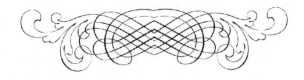

Homemade Ketchup (Slow Cooked)

Serves: 48

In terms of sugar, ketchup is one of the worst condiments you can have. It's also one of the most versatile - what is a hot dog without ketchup? Luckily, you can make your own with just a little sugar, and lots of spices like onion powder, cloves, and paprika. It tastes just like the store-bought, but it keeps getting better over time. In the fridge, it lasts 10 days, and freezes for up to 2 months.

Cooking Note: It's best to start this recipe during the morning and be home all day, because it requires stirring.

Prep time: 1 minute
Cook time: 10-12 hours
Blend time: 5 minutes
Total time: 10 hours, 6 minutes – 12 hours, 6 minutes

Ingredients:

2 (28-ounce) cans of peeled tomatoes
½ cup water
¼ cup white sugar
¾ cup white vinegar
1 teaspoon onion powder
½ teaspoon ground cloves
½ teaspoon garlic powder
½ teaspoon paprika
¼ teaspoon black pepper
⅛ teaspoon mustard powder
Salt to taste

Instructions:

1. Grease Crock-Pot.
2. Add tomatoes and water.
3. Add all the spices and stir well.
4. Close the lid.
5. Hit SLOW COOK and cook for 10-12 hours on low, stirring at least every 2 hours.
6. When time is up, puree until smooth.
7. To get rid of any seeds, pour through a strainer.
8. Keep in an airtight container in the fridge when not using!

Nutritional Info (1/48 serving):
Total calories: 16
Protein: 0
Carbs: 4
Fat: 0
Fiber: 0

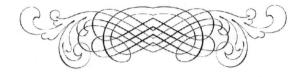

Habanero Hot Sauce (Pressure Cooked)

<u>Makes:</u> 20-ounces

Prep time: 5 minutes
Cook time: 3 minutes
Natural pressure release: 10 minutes
Blend time: 5 minutes
Total time: 23 minutes

Habanero peppers have a slightly-sweet flavor to their heat, which is why I love this hot sauce. The shredded carrots add a little sweetness as well, but don't think that this hot sauce isn't *hot*. As a reference, habaneros are much hotter than jalapenos. Other flavors you'll get from this include the smokiness of a roasted red pepper and acid from white vinegar, apple cider vinegar, and lime juice. This sauce goes well on everything!

Ingredients:

1 pound habanero peppers
¼ cup shredded carrots
3 teaspoons ground garlic
1 chopped roasted red pepper
1 cup white vinegar
⅛ cup apple cider vinegar
⅛ cup lime juice
½ cup water
1 tablespoon salt

Instructions:

1. Cut off pepper tops and chop each one into three pieces.
2. Put in your Crock-Pot.

3. Add the rest of the ingredients.
4. Seal the lid.
5. Hit STEAM and adjust time to 3 minutes.
6. When time is up, wait for a natural pressure release.
7. Carefully open the lid to cool, avoiding hot pepper fumes.
8. When cool, blend until smooth.
9. Strain into bottles.
10. Store in fridge when not using!

Nutritional Info (1 ounce serving):
Total calories: 92
Protein: 5
Carbs: 24
Fat: 0
Fiber: 0

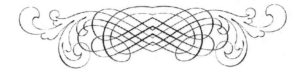

Serrano Relish (Slow Cooked)

<u>Makes:</u> 3 cups

Prep time: 5 minutes
Cook time: 3-4 hours
Pulse time: 5 minutes
Total time: 3 hours, 10 minutes – 4 hours, 10 minutes

Relish is a versatile condiment that can go on everything from hot dogs to chicken. What I love about this recipe is that it's both spicy and sweet. Good food has more than one flavor profile going on. Serrano chiles are spicier than jalapenos, with a sharp bite. That gets mellowed by cooking, and sweetened with sugar.

Cooking Note: To store, keep the relish in the fridge for up to 2 weeks.

<u>Ingredients:</u>

1 big sweet onion
30 serrano chiles
2 green bell peppers
1 cup apple cider vinegar
½ cup white sugar
1 teaspoon salt

<u>Instructions:</u>

1. Peel and slice onion in half.
2. Remove the stem from all the chiles and the bell peppers.
3. Chop bell peppers, and leave the chiles whole.
4. Toss onion, chiles, and peppers into your Crock-Pot.

5. Pour in apple cider vinegar, sugar, and salt.
6. Close the lid.
7. Hit SLOW COOK and cook on HIGH for 3-4 hours.
8. When time is up, open the lid and move to a food processor.
9. Pulse until you get the texture you want.

Nutritional Info (½ cup serving):
Total calories: 93
Protein: 2
Carbs: 23
Fat: 0
Fiber: 1.6

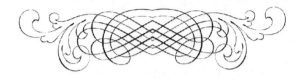

Caramelized Onions (Pressure Cooked)

<u>Makes:</u> 3 cups

Prep time: 10 minutes
Cook time: 20 minutes
Natural pressure release: 5 minutes
Additional time: 10 minutes
Total time: 45 minutes

Sticky-sweet, caramel-colored onions are amazing on top of just about everything, from hamburgers to chicken breasts to pork chops. You may think of it as a traditional "condiment," but after you've made them yourself using the Multi-Cooker's pressure cooking setting, you'll understand why they're here. If you don't eat them all right away, they last 10 days in the fridge.

Cooking Note: Baking powder helps activate the process that gives cooked onions that caramelized, sticky quality.

<u>Ingredients:</u>

2 pounds peeled and thinly-sliced sweet onions
½ teaspoon baking powder
6 tablespoons butter
Salt to taste
Black pepper to taste

<u>Instructions:</u>

1. Grease your Crock-Pot.
2. In a bowl, mix onions and baking powder.
3. Turn your Crock-Pot to BROWN/SAUTÉ and add butter.

4. When melted, add onions.
5. Stir until onions are beginning to soften.
6. Season and seal the lid.
7. Hit BEANS/CHILI and adjust time to 20 minutes on high pressure.
8. When time is up, wait 5 minutes, and then quick-release the pressure.
9. Turn your Crock-Pot back on to BROWN/SAUTÉ and stir, until cooking liquid has reduced.
10. Onions should be deep brown and caramelized!

Nutritional Info (½ cup serving):
Total calories: 150
Protein: 1
Carbs: 11
Fat: 12
Fiber: 2.6

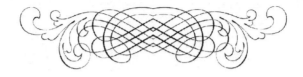

Bacon Jam (Slow Cooked)

<u>Serves:</u> 8

Prep time: 15 minutes
Cook time: 4 hours
Pulse time: 5 minutes
Total time: 4 hours, 20 minutes

Often considered a "gourmet" condiment, bacon jam is actually really easy and affordable to make yourself. It's infused with amazingly-rich, deep, salty, sweet, and smoky flavors that go really well with hamburgers, in mashed potatoes, and in pasta dishes. Every ingredient plays a role in building that flavor profile. Take note that this is actually a rare recipe where you cook the whole time *with the lid off*.

Ingredients:

1 pound chopped bacon
2 chopped red onions
3 minced garlic cloves
3 tablespoons brown sugar
¾ cup brewed coffee
4 tablespoons pure maple syrup
½ cup apple cider vinegar
1 tablespoon balsamic vinegar

Instructions:

1. Turn your Crock-Pot to BROWN/SAUTÉ and add bacon.
2. Fry until browned and beginning to crisp.
3. Remove and plate on a paper towel for now.
4. Add onions and garlic into your Crock-Pot with the leftover bacon

5. fat, and cook until onions turn clear.
5. Stir in sugar, coffee, maple syrup, and apple cider vinegar, and deglaze, scraping up any stuck-on food bits.
6. When boiling, return bacon to the Crock-Pot and stir.
7. Do *not* close the lid, but do cook on SLOW COOK for 4 hours on HIGH.
8. When the jam has become thick and syrupy, add balsamic vinegar.
9. Blend in a food processor to get the texture you want.
10. It's ready!

Nutritional Info (⅛ serving):
Total calories: 301
Protein: 16
Carbs: 13
Fat: 22
Fiber: 0

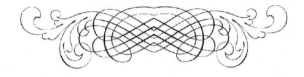

Maple-Chipotle BBQ Sauce (Pressure Cooked)

Makes: 2 ½ cups

Prep time: 15 minutes
Cook time: 10 minutes
Pulse time: 5 minutes
Total time: 30 minutes

There are countless BBQ sauce brands out there, and they vary widely in quality. Making your own is easy and usually healthier, since you can control what ingredients go into it. For a quick but delicious sauce that goes well on any kind of protein, you use the pressure cooking setting on the Multi-Cooker. Thanks to chipotle powder, the sauce gets a smoky flavor that usually only comes from long cooking times. Maple syrup and prunes add sweetness, while acidity comes from a healthy serving of apple cider vinegar.

Ingredients:

1 tablespoon extra-virgin olive oil
1 chopped onion
½ cup water
½ cup tomato puree
4 tablespoons maple syrup
4 tablespoons apple cider vinegar

1 teaspoon salt
½ teaspoon ground garlic
1 teaspoon hot sauce
1 teaspoon chipotle powder
¼ teaspoon cumin
¾ cup prunes

Instructions:

1. Turn your Crock-Pot to BROWN/SAUTÉ.
2. Add oil.
3. When hot, add onion and cook until beginning to turn golden.
4. Turn off the Crock-Pot.
5. Pour in water, tomato puree, maple syrup, and vinegar.
6. Add salt, garlic, hot sauce, chipotle, and cumin.
7. Mix, until maple syrup and tomato puree have dissolved.
8. Add prunes and seal the lid.
9. Hit BEANS/CHILI and adjust time to 10 minutes on high pressure.
10. When time is up, quick-release the pressure.
11. Use a food processor or immersion blender to get the BBQ sauce texture you want.
12. For the best flavor, store in the fridge in an airtight container overnight, to let the flavors really blend.

Nutritional Info (½ cup serving):
Total calories: 150
Protein: 1
Carbs: 30
Fat: 3
Fiber: 2

Chapter 13: Desserts

Making desserts is one of my favorite ways to use the Express Multi-Cooker. There's no end to the variety of goodies I can make, from cakes to custards to crisps. Cakes and scones can be cooked right in the pot without the need for extra bowls, while some recipes basically use the cooker to steam custard and fruit. Whether you prefer to use the slow cooker function on your Express all the time, or the pressure cooker setting, you'll find great options in this section for every occasion.

Chocolate Chip + Orange Scones (Slow Cooked)	*212*
Pumpkin Pie (Slow Cooked)	*214*
Apple-Pear Crisp (Slow Cooked)	*216*
Chocolate Molten Cake (Slow Cooked)	*218*
Cinnamon-Raisin Bread Pudding (Slow Cooked)	*220*
Classic Cheesecake (Pressure Cooked)	*222*
Date-Night Fudge Cake (Pressure Cooked)	*225*
Black 'n Blue Cobbler (Pressure Cooked)	*227*
Rich Lemon Custard (Pressure Cooked)	*229*
Cider-Poached Pears w/ Cinnamon-Pecan Syrup (Pressure Cooked)	*231*

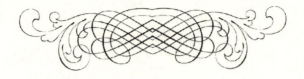

Chocolate Chip + Orange Scones (Slow Cooked)

Serves: 8

Prep time: 7 minutes
Cook time: 1 hour, 30 minutes
Total time: 1 hour, 37 minutes

I have fond memories of making scones with my sister when I was a kid. My favorite always had chocolate chips in them. Making scones in the Crock-Pot is easy. Simply mix the dry ingredients and cut in butter, like you do for biscuits, and add milk. Once this is mixed in a sticky dough, add "extras," which in this recipe are chocolate chips and orange zest. Make sure your Crock-Pot is greased really well (or use a liner), and put in your dough to bake for 1 ½ hours.

Ingredients:

1 ½ cups flour
1 ½ teaspoons baking powder
½ teaspoon salt
¼ cup sugar
¼ cup butter
Just over ½ cup milk
⅔ cup chocolate chips
1 tablespoon orange zest

Instructions:

1. Line your Crock-Pot or grease really well.
2. Mix flour, baking powder, salt, and sugar together in a bowl.

3. Cut in the butter to get a crumbly texture.
4. Add milk and stir. You'll get a soft dough.
5. Add chocolate chips and orange zest.
6. Form with your hands into a round cake.
7. Stick the dough into the Crock-Pot.
8. Hit SLOW COOK and cook on the high temp setting for 1 ½ hours.
9. Carefully remove from the pot and cool.
10. Slice into triangles.

Nutritional Info (1 scone):
Total calories: 247
Protein: 5
Carbs: 34
Fat: 12
Fiber: 0

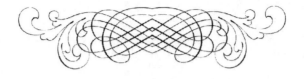

Pumpkin Pie (Slow Cooked)

Serves: 6-8

Prep time: 7 minutes
Cook time: 1 hour, 30 minutes
Total time: 1 hour, 37 minutes

Pie can be a challenge if you aren't an experienced baker. The crust is the hardest part, so for this Crock-Pot recipe, you're not bothering with it at all. It's almost more like a custard than a pie. Mix all the ingredients right in your greased Crock-Pot and bake for 2-4 hours, until it's set. Don't forget the whipped cream!

Ingredients:

15-ounces canned pumpkin
2 beaten eggs
2 tablespoons melted butter
¾ cup brown sugar
½ cup flour
12-ounces evaporated milk
½ teaspoon baking powder
¼ teaspoon salt
2 teaspoons pumpkin pie spice

Instructions:

1. Line your Crock-Pot or grease really well.
2. In the Crock-Pot, mix all the ingredients.
3. Close the lid.
4. Hit SLOW COOK and cook on the low setting for 2-4 hours, until set.

5. Serve with whipped cream!

Nutritional Info (⅙ recipe):
Total calories: 240
Protein: 9
Carbs: 38
Fat: 7
Fiber: 0

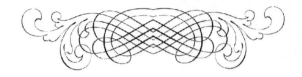

Apple-Pear Crisp (Slow Cooked)

Serves: 6-8

Prep time: 7 minutes
Cook time: 4 hours
Total time: 4 hours, 7 minutes

I've always liked adding different fruits to apple crisp to give the dessert more layers of flavor. Pear goes really well with tart apples. Lay the sliced and peeled fruit down in your greased Crock-Pot, and then mix the streusel topping together. Sprinkle evenly over the fruit, and "bake" for 4 hours on the low setting. You get the perfect autumn dessert - sweet from the fruit juices, and crisp and buttery on top.

Ingredients:

4 peeled and sliced tart apples
2 peeled and sliced ripe pears
⅔ cup rolled oats
⅔ cup flour
⅔ cup light brown sugar
1 teaspoon cinnamon
½ teaspoon nutmeg
Pinch of salt
½ cup butter

Instructions:

1. Line or grease the bottom of your Crock-Pot really well.
2. Put the sliced fruit on the bottom.
3. In a bowl, mix oats, flour, brown sugar, and spices.

4. Cut in the butter, so it becomes crumbly.
5. Add to the Crock-Pot over the fruit.
6. Lay paper towels on top, and then put the lid on.
7. Hit SLOW COOK and cook on the low setting for 4 hours.
8. Serve!

Nutritional Info (⅙ recipe):
Total calories: 292
Protein: 3
Carbs: 43
Fat: 16
Fiber: 4.8

CHAPTER 13: DESSERTS

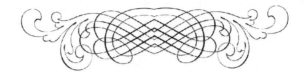

Chocolate Molten Cake (Slow Cooked)

Serves: 4-6

Prep time: 7 minutes
Cook time: 2-3 hours
Cool time: 30 minutes
Total time: 2 hours, 37 minutes – 3 hours, 37 minutes

Chocolate molten cake - also known as a lava cake - has a very specific process, so you end up with a liquidy chocolate center. You can make it right in your Crock-Pot in less than 4 hours. Mix the cake part first, and then pour the chocolate center part on top, making sure to not stir. That's what gives the cake its molten middle.

Cooking Note: Make sure to use Dutch-processed cocoa.

Ingredients:

1 cup flour
2 teaspoons baking powder
6 tablespoons butter
2-ounces chocolate chips
⅔ cup sugar
3 tablespoons cocoa powder
1 tablespoon pure vanilla
¼ teaspoon salt
⅓ cup milk
1 egg yolk
⅓ cup white sugar
⅓ cup brown sugar
⅓ cup cocoa powder

1 ½ cups hot water

Instructions:

1. Grease your Crock-Pot really well, or insert liner.
2. In a bowl, mix flour and baking powder.
3. In another bowl, melt butter and chocolate in the microwave in 30-second periods, mixing between times.
4. When melted, add in sugar, cocoa, vanilla, salt, milk, and egg yolk.
5. Add the dry into this bowl and mix well.
6. Pour into Crock-Pot and spread evenly.
7. In a second bowl, whisk sugar, brown sugar, cocoa, and hot water.
8. Pour over the batter, but DO NOT MIX.
9. Close the lid.
10. Hit SLOW COOK and cook for 2-3 hours on the high setting, checking after 2 hours. Cake should look cooked, with the edges beginning to pull away from the Crock-Pot sides.
11. Cool for 30 minutes before serving!

Nutritional Info (¼ recipe):
Total calories: 601
Protein: 8
Carbs: 97
Fat: 25
Fiber: 0

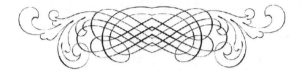

Cinnamon-Raisin Bread Pudding (Slow Cooked)

Serves: 8

Prep time: 15 minutes
Cook time: 2 ½-3 hours
Total time: 2 hours, 45 minutes - 3 hours, 15 minutes

Need a brunch for a crowd? For a really decadent dish, try this cinnamon-raisin bread pudding. It serves 8 people and can be made in the morning hours before guests arrive. The prep time includes the 10 minutes needed for the bread to soak in milk, eggs, sugar, butter, and spices. Check the doneness of the pudding like it's a cake - a clean toothpick means it's ready

Cooking Note: The best bread pudding is made from sturdy bread, like Brioche and French bread. If you think your bread might be too soft, stick it in a 350-degree oven for 15-20 minutes to dry it out.

Ingredients:

6 cups of cubed cinnamon-raisin bread
½ cup raisins
2 cups milk
4 eggs
1 cup sugar
¼ cup melted butter
1 teaspoon ground cinnamon
½ teaspoon pure vanilla
½ teaspoon nutmeg

Instructions:

1. Grease your Crock-Pot really well, or insert a liner.
2. Put down the bread and raisins inside.
3. In a bowl, mix milk, eggs, sugar, butter, cinnamon, vanilla, and nutmeg together.
4. Pour over bread and raisins.
5. With a spoon, mix around, so bread cubes get soaked.
6. Wait 10 minutes.
7. Mix around again before closing the lid.
8. Cook on SLOW COOK on the low setting for 2 ½-3 hours, checking after 2 ½ hours. A toothpick should come out of the center clean.
9. Serve warm!

Nutritional Info (⅛ recipe):
Total calories: 327
Protein: 13
Carbs: 55
Fat: 11
Fiber: 0

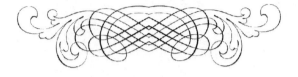

Classic Cheesecake (Pressure Cooked)

Serves: 6

Prep time: 20-30 minutes
Cook time: 26 minutes
Natural pressure release: 7 minutes
Cool time: 15-20 minutes
Chill time: 6 hours
Total time: 7 hours, 8 minutes - 7 hours, 23 minutes

I didn't consider myself a *real* cook until I could make a cheesecake from scratch. This is the most classic of classics recipes, with a graham-cracker crust and silky-smooth filling. There are two ways to make the crust - one that's baked and one that isn't. It's up to you which you prefer. There are a lot of instructions, so it looks intimidating, but I've just really broken down the process to help you out. Thanks to the Crock-Pot Express, "baking" only takes 26 minutes!

Cooking Note: Use a hand mixer to mix cheesecake, but it can quickly become over-whipped. If you don't have one, use the lowest possible setting on your standing mixer and watch very carefully.

Ingredients:

10 ground graham crackers
½ tablespoon brown sugar
¼ cup flour
3-4 tablespoons melted butter

2 tablespoons cornstarch
Pinch of salt

⅔ cup white sugar
16-ounces room temperature cream cheese
½ cup room-temperature sour cream
2 teaspoons pure vanilla
2 room-temperature eggs

1 cup cold water

Instructions:

1. Begin with the crust. In a bowl, mix graham cracker crumbs with brown sugar.
2. Mix in flour.
3. Add butter until the mixture becomes a bit sticky.
4. Line a cheesecake pan with parchment paper, so it comes up the sides, too.
5. Press in the crust on the bottom and up the sides.
6. Stick in a 325-degree oven for 15 minutes.

Cooking Note: If you don't want to bake your crust, leave out the flour, and then freeze while you're making the cheesecake batter.

7. Now for the batter! Mix cornstarch, salt, and white sugar in a bowl.
8. In another bowl, beat the cream cheese for just *10 seconds* with a hand mixer. You want to be very careful not to over-whip.
9. Add in half of your sugar mixture and beat for 20-30 seconds. Add the rest and beat again for another 20-30 seconds.
10. Slowly beat in the sour cream and vanilla until just incorporated.
11. Lastly, add one egg and beat until mixed. Add the remaining egg and mix.
12. Pour batter into your crust.
13. To get rid of air bubbles, tap the pan against the counter, and then pop bubbles.
14. Pour cold water into your Crock-Pot and lower in trivet.
15. Put the cheesecake pan on the trivet and seal the lid.
16. Hit BEANS/CHILI and cook on high pressure for 26 minutes.
17. When time is up, wait for 7 minutes and then quick-release any leftover pressure.
18. Remove the lid and wait until cheesecake is at room-temperature before removing.
19. Cool for another 10-15 minutes.
20. Remove the cheesecake pan sides (leaving the bottom on) and chill in the fridge for at least 6 hours.

21. Remove bottom of the pan and serve!

Nutritional Info (⅙ recipe):
Total calories: 604
Protein: 10
Carbs: 49
Fat: 43
Fiber: 0

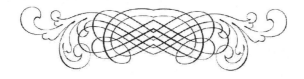

Date-Night Fudge Cake (Pressure Cooked)

Serves: 2

Prep time: 7 minutes
Cook time: 10 minutes
Cool time: 5 minutes
Total time: 22 minutes

Every good date needs a good dessert. This rich fudge cake takes only 22 minutes total, so you don't spend much time apart from your special someone. Simply melt chocolate in a bowl, mix in butter and egg, and then dry ingredients. Pour into two ramekins, and put in your Crock-Pot. Two cups of water generate the steam on the pressure cooker setting, which you adjust to just 10 minutes.

Ingredients:

½ cup chocolate chips
1 tablespoon butter
1 egg
1 ½ teaspoons sugar
1 teaspoon flour
Pinch of sea salt
2 cups water

Instructions:

1. In a microwave-safe bowl, melt chocolate.
2. Mix in butter until incorporated.
3. Mix in the egg.
4. Add sugar, flour, and salt and stir well.
5. Grease two ramekins and pour in batter, so each ramekin is about

½ full.
6. Pour water into your Crock-Pot.
7. Lay down a trivet.
8. Put ramekins on the trivet and seal the lid.
9. Hit BEANS/CHILI and cook for 10 minutes on high pressure.
10. When time is up, turn off the Crock-Pot and quick-release the pressure.
11. Take out the ramekins and cool for 5 minutes.
12. Serve as is, or with a scoop of ice cream!

Nutritional Info (½ recipe):
Total calories: 379
Protein: 7
Carbs: 39
Fat: 27
Fiber: 0

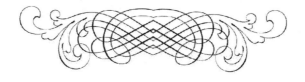

Black 'n Blue Cobbler (Pressure Cooked)

Serves: 4

Prep time: 5 minutes
Cook time: 25 minutes
Natural pressure release: 10 minutes
Total time: 40 minutes

Named for both blueberries and blackberries, this pressure cooked cobbler is just the right amount of sweet. The filling is berries, sugar, lemon juice, vanilla, and cornstarch, while the topping is flour, baking powder, brown sugar, butter, and milk. Cook on high pressure for 25 minutes, and then wait for a natural pressure release to ensure the topping cooks through.

Ingredients:

1 cup frozen blackberries
1 cup frozen blueberries
1 cup sugar
⅛ cup lemon juice
1 teaspoon pure vanilla
1 teaspoon cornstarch

2 cups flour
1 tablespoon baking powder
½ cup brown sugar
¼ cup melted butter
1 cup milk

Instructions:

1. Grease your Crock-Pot really well or insert liner.
2. Start by making the filling. Mix all the ingredients in the first list together.
3. To make the topping, mix everything from the second ingredient list in a bowl.
4. Pour over the filling and spread flat with a spatula.
5. Seal the lid.
6. Cook on BEANS/CHILI on high pressure for 25 minutes.
7. When time is up, turn off the Crock-Pot and wait for a natural pressure release.
8. Serve!

Nutritional Info (¼ recipe):
Total calories: 539
Protein: 7
Carbs: 101
Fat: 15
Fiber: 2.75

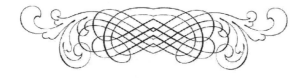

Rich Lemon Custard (Pressure Cooked)

<u>Serves:</u> 6

Prep time: 36 minutes
Cook time: 10 minutes
Natural pressure release: 10 minutes
Cool time: 30-45 minutes
Chill time: 2 hours
Total time: 3 hours, 26 minutes - 3 hours, 41 minutes

This is one of the longer pressure cooking recipes, but only because it needs a 2-hour chill time. If you aren't a huge fan of chocolate or just want something on the citrusy side, cold lemon custard hits the spot. Milk, cream, and lemon zest simmer together on the stove until boiling, and then cools for 20-30 minutes. Egg and sugar get mixed together in a separate bowl, and once the cream is cool, pour into the egg and sugar. The custard cooks in 6 ramekins wrapped in foil.

Cooking Note: You can serve with any kind of fruit you want, because lemon goes with everything.

<u>*Ingredients:*</u>

1 cup whole milk
1 cup heavy cream
1 lemon's worth of zest
6 egg yolks
⅔ cup sugar
1 cup water
1 cup fresh raspberries

Instructions:

1. Heat a saucepan on medium, and add milk, cream, and lemon zest.
2. Simmer together until it begins to boil.
3. Quickly remove from the heat and wait 20-30 minutes.
4. While that cools, mix egg yolks and sugar in a bowl until smooth.
5. When the cream mixture is cool, pour slowly into your egg mixture.
6. Whisk until just incorporated; you aren't whipping this.
7. Pour into 6 greased ramekins and cover with foil.
8. Pour water into your Crock-Pot and lower in trivet.
9. Put ramekins on the trivet and seal the lid.
10. Hit BEANS/CHILI and cook on high pressure for 10 minutes.
11. When time is up, wait for a natural pressure release.
12. Custard will be set, not liquidy. Take off the foil and cool for 30-45 minutes at room temperature.
13. Cover with saran wrap and chill in the fridge for 2 hours or so.
14. To serve, top with fresh raspberries!

Nutritional Info (⅙ recipe):

Total calories: 200
Protein: 4
Carbs: 25
Fat: 10
Fiber: 2.6

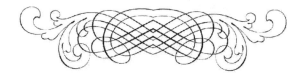

Cider-Poached Pears w/ Cinnamon-Pecan Syrup (Pressure Cooked)

Serves: 4

Prep time: 5 minutes
Cook time: 8 minutes
Natural pressure release: 10 minutes
Syrup time: 12 minutes
Total time: 35 minutes

With only five ingredients, this fruit dessert is infused with sweetness, cinnamon, and nutty flavors. By cooking pears in apple cider and cinnamon sticks, they become super soft and sweet, while the apple cider turns into a syrup that's made even more delicious with pecans and a sprinkle of sea salt.

Ingredients:

1 cup apple cider
4 peeled pears
2 cinnamon sticks
½ cup chopped pecans
Sprinkle of sea salt

Instructions:

1. Pour cider into your Crock-Pot.
2. Cut a slice off the bottom of the pears, so they stand up on their own. Lay them down on their sides in the Crock-Pot.
3. Toss in cinnamon sticks.

4. Seal the lid.
5. Hit BEANS/CHILI and cook for 8 minutes on high pressure.
6. When time is up, wait for a natural pressure release.
7. Take out the pears and plate for now.
8. To make the syrup, turn your Crock-Pot to BROWN/SAUTÉ and let the mixture come to a boil.
9. Boil until the liquid gets a syrupy consistency.
10. When ready, turn off the Crock-Pot, remove the cinnamon sticks, and stir in chopped pecans and salt.
11. Serve pears with cinnamon cider-pecan syrup drizzled on top!

Nutritional Info (¼ recipe):
Total calories: 229
Protein: 2
Carbs: 37
Fat: 10
Fiber: 7

Epilogue

There's nothing like the feeling of making a good meal for loved ones. It's my love language, and I know that many of you speak that same language. Sadly, life can get chaotic and it becomes difficult to take the time to cook. That's why appliances like the Express Multi-Cooker are so valuable: they make cooking more convenient.

In this book, you learned all about the Multi-Cooker, and how it's different from other devices. In addition to the low-and-slow cooking function that has defined Crock-Pot for years, it's also a pressure cooker. That means meals get done faster and have more nutrients preserved, which is the best possible news for people wanting to break their fast-food and takeout habit. The Multi-Cooker's versatility means you can cook just about any kind of food, as the recipe portion of the book proved. There were chicken dishes, hearty pot roasts, savory seafood, and decadent desserts. There are even a handful of condiments you can make in the cooker, like ketchup and relish, so you save money and enjoy a healthier version than what you get in the store.

My goal with this book was to provide information and recipe inspiration for everyone. What I love about cooking is that there's always something new to learn, and new flavors to experience. Hopefully you've learned and experienced something new!